Y0-BZB-457

To Hernando
Paredes

in appreciation

from
Art Robertson

The Language of Effective Listening

The ScottForesman
Applications in Management
Series

ROBERT B. NELSON,
Editor

The Language of Effective Listening

Arthur K. Robertson

ScottForesman
ProfessionalBooks

An Imprint of ScottForesman

To my son, Scott, an excellent listener.

First Printing, 1991

Carmel, Indiana 46032
Copyright © 1991 by Arthur K. Robertson

All rights reserved. No part of this work shall be
reproduced, stored in a retrieval system, or transmitted by
any means, electronic, mechanical, photocopying, recording, or
otherwise, without written permission from the publisher. No
patent liability is assumed with respect to the use of the
information contained herein. While every precaution has been
taken in the preparation of this work, the publisher and
author assume no responsibility for errors or omissions.
Neither is any liability assumed for damages resulting from
the use of the information contained herein.

Editorial services by BooksCraft, Inc., Indianapolis.

Library of Congress Cataloging-in-Publication Data

Robertson, Arthur K.
    The language of effective listening / Arthur K. Robertson.
        p.   cm. — (The ScottForesman applications in management
    series)
    Includes bibliographical references and index.
    ISBN 0-673-46333-8
    1. Business communication. 2. Listening. 3. Interpersonal com-
    munication.   I. Title.   II. Series: ScottForesman applications in
    management series.
    HF5718.R59   1991
    658.4'52—dc20   91-9114
                                                                          CIP

Printed in the United States of America.

CONTENTS

Series Foreword

The ScottForesman Applications in Management Series provides short, practical, easy-to-read books about basic business skills.

Low on theory and high on practical techniques and examples, this series addresses the key skill areas needed to be a successful manager in business today. It supplies specific answers to questions you have and offers new approaches to problems you face in your job.

Each book in the series is written by one or more individuals who have extensive, first-hand experience in the topic being discussed. The drafted books are then reviewed by several front-line managers to ensure that each meets their needs in delivering practical, useful information in a format that is easy to understand and use.

I am confident that this book—and others in the AIM series—will provide you with tips and techniques to enable you to do your job better today and in the future.

Robert B. Nelson
Series Editor

Foreword

Don't be misled by the title of Art Robertson's *The Language of Effective Listening*. It is about a lot more than how to hear better. Effective listening engages all the senses. This book is a landmark work on the most needed, yet most ignored, communication skill. Effective communication is the foundation for all relationships, both professional and personal. Effective listening is the key that unlocks the door to communication, positive relationships, and maximum productivity.

In 1980, after I heard about Art Robertson's successful programs for AT & T and IBM, I invited him to attend one of our Situational Leadership training sessions in Philadelphia. We drove back to New York together and have been friends and colleagues ever since.

Frequently we discuss the importance of effective listening in the life of a One Minute Manager. More than half of an effective manager's time is spent listening. Several books have been written about listening, but never before has one volume pulled together the basic elements of listening as a language skill with such a solid, conceptual base, while being profoundly practical. Practicing what this book teaches will be a breakthrough for building positive relationships among colleagues, employees, and clients, and for maximizing productivity. Relationships with family and friends will be rekindled.

Listening, as Art teaches, is an assertive act of extracting the information you need to manage or sell or live more effectively. For the most part, people *want* to tell you what they need. Your challenge in management, in sales, and in life is to help bring out those needs, evaluate them, and fashion a response that helps you come out ahead.

Dr. Robertson teaches this listening process in his exciting workshop. Now you have it at your fingertips with *The Language of Effective Listening*. Art's exciting, dynamic, and sometimes humorous writing drive home his message.

Practice the methods Art teaches and you will raise the self-esteem of your colleagues and family members. You will learn how to become specific in setting observable, measurable, and obtainable communication goals. Effective listening is the language of effective persons. You will become a more effective listener, a more effective manager or professional, and a more effective family member and friend.

An exciting element of the Language of Effective Listening is that you already know more than you practice. Much of this important skill, already hidden in your subconscious, is waiting to be brought to awareness by this book. Practice what you read and you will learn what thousands of workshop participants have learned. It works. I think you will enjoy reading Art Robertson's *The Language of Effective Listening*. I'm confident you will profit by it. I know I did.

Ken Blanchard
Author, *The One Minute Manager*

Acknowledgements

I am grateful to Mary Ann Orman who, in 1978 while on staff at AT & T, telephoned and invited me to research, develop, and present an effective listening workshop to AT & T corporate managers. In doing so, I underwent the metamorphosis of becoming a more effective listener and prepared myself to share the methodology with others, which I have enjoyed immensely.

My program would not have been successful without the generous contribution of "The Ambassador of Listening," Dr. Lyman K. Steil. "Manny" taught the listening courses at the University of Minnesota, and is now the president of Communication Development, Inc., St. Paul, Minnesota. Manny gave me the opportunity to learn from his academic research in effective listening. He gave me the benefit of his own practical experience, always embellished with his outstanding character. He guaranteed that this willing disciple would be successful in learning and teaching the important skill of effective listening. Thank you Manny!

In addition, I am very thankful to the thousands of managers and professionals at IBM, AT & T, and the many other Fortune 100 companies who responded enthusiastically to my teaching methods and materials. I learned as much from listening to them as they did from listening to me.

Thanks also to Dr. Ken Boa for his numerous insights and encouragement as a teaching colleague. Thanks to Roger Petersen for the humorous touch, and his drawings of the various facial expressions. A special thanks to Dr. Jay Sidebotham for his excellent cartoons sprinkled throughout the text. Thanks to Bill Proctor for faithfully reflecting my thoughts in the beginning and concluding parables.

I am indebted to several who gave thoughtful and helpful criticism to the early manuscript. They deserve credit for clarity and accuracy of the text. Where problems or mistakes still exist, I take full responsibility for not always following their advice. Sincere thanks are extended to Dr. Suzette Haden Elgin, professor of psycholinguistics emeritus, San Diego State College; Dr. Bernard G. Guerney, Jr., professor of human development at Pennsylvania State University and head of the Individual and Family Consultation Center; Tom Taylor, professor of biblical languages at Biblical Theological Seminary; Tom Dunkerton, retired senior vice-president of Saatchi, Saatchi and Compton; Lourene Clark, vice president, executive development at Citicorp; and Joe Moore, manager of human resources at R. R. Donnelley.

Many thanks to Stephany Hull, who took time from an already busy schedule and worked long hours over a very short period to craft my first draft into a respectable manuscript. And then persisted to the end by editing numerous other drafts until the current document was completed.

I am grateful to Ms. Amy Davis for giving me the opportunity to write this book, and for her gracious encouragement as the deadline approached.

Bob Nelson, series editor, told me of the opportunity to write this book and then advised, tactfully admonished, and encouraged me to complete it. Thanks to Maria Schapker. Her editorial role in the final draft has helped considerably.

Most of all, thanks to my wonderful wife, Linda, a true woman of Proverbs thirty-one, "who is more precious than jewels." Her love, prayers, dedication, and support made it possible for me to leave a secure college teaching position and embark on the successful adventure of learning and teaching these skills in the corporate community. Linda has taught me to listen to the heart as well as to the mind.

Introduction

Speaking to the Financial Analysts Federation General Session, the former labor secretary, Ray Donovan, shared an early experience in investing. "I've learned that you have to listen very carefully to what financial analysts and investment advisors tell you. This comes as a result of twenty-five years experience with advisors, many of whom are in this room, I'm sure. But, I did have a meeting with my investment advisor back in the good old days before I entered the government. I had some money to invest, and I asked him if a particular investment was a good idea. He says, 'Ray, you stand to make a lot of money out of that investment.'"

"I thanked him. I went back home. I discussed it with my wife and put a fairly large sum of money into the deal. In six weeks I lost every penny of it. So I went back to that advisor, and I started to complain about the advice he gave. He looked me straight in the eye and said, 'Ray, I gave you good advice. The trouble is you just didn't listen. I said you'd make money *out* of that deal, not in it.'"

Ineffective listening costs money!

Effective listening is the number one communication skill requisite to success in your professional and personal life. Yet, in our hurry-up society, pressure mounts to get more things done in less time, so it has never been more difficult to be an effective listener.

Approximately 70 percent of our Fortune 500 companies have listening training programs, but 70 percent of the managers in those companies are perceived to be only fair listeners. This book was written to guide you through the successful process that has helped thousands of managers and professionals become more effective listeners. Our listening program lets participants translate what they learn from this book into real-life applications at work and at home.

Language is defined in the *Oxford American Dictionary* as a system of signs and symbols used to convey information. Through "The Language of Effective Listening," the effective listener conveys to the speaker an understanding of the speaker's message. This self-help book is for people who want to improve their communication with the significant people in their lives. By reading just twenty minutes each day, you will gain sufficient new techniques to immediately apply in your regular communication activities. We will help you identify skills to practice in the real world. The *payoff* comes with practice.

Many of the principles will strike you as new. But others that *seem* new have been previously learned and locked in your subconscious. Reading and reflection will bring to your conscious awareness what you have subconsciously stored in your memory. By reflecting and practicing the exercises provided, your level of awareness of effective listening skills will increase. This sense of familiarity will raise your level of comfort with the material, and make it easier to apply.

To help yourself, you will be asked to identify five people with whom you would like to build better communication. Choose some from your professional environment and others from your personal relationships. Think of these five people consistently as you read the book. Immediately following a reading session, try to practice the skills you have learned when communicating with these individuals. By applying what the book teaches, you increase your potential for success.

Frequently, humorous anecdotes illustrate a principle. Learning is more enjoyable and, therefore, much easier if you are able to laugh once in a while. The ancient theory that laughter is good medicine actually has a physiological basis. The *American Medical Association Bulletin* reports that every organ of the body responds to laughter. According to *American Health,* it works this way. ". . . the pituitary gland shoots out endorphins, chemical cousins of such painkilling drugs as heroin and morphine. Lachrymal glands of the eyes produce tears. The zygomatic muscles in the head contort as if in pain. The lower jaw vibrates lickety-bang. The arteries relax after tensing. Vocal cords undergo spasms and produce sound. The heart increases its pace, meeting immediate oxygen needs. Lungs build pressure before releasing air. The diaphragm tightens for spasms of respiration. From the nervous system comes a deluge of adrenaline, which ensue in euphoria. Abdominal muscles double like a fist. Leg muscles relax, causing a weakening feeling." Science is only in the preliminary stages of isolating the tremendous benefits of laughter.

Laughter is a metaphor for the entire range of positive emotions: faith, hope, love, the will to live, cheer, humor, creativity, playfulness, confidence, and great expectations. Positive thoughts are the launching pad for making healthy relationships at work and at home. Healthy relationships increase productivity. Happy people laugh about four hundred times a day.

The positive feelings that ensue from a moment of laughter are fleeting. The positive results from using the Language of Effective Listening with the most significant people in your life will last. So, the jokes and cartoons are an attempt to keep you moving toward the greater benefits. As John the apostle said, "We are writing that your joy may be complete."

The parable of chapter 1 is a compilation of bits and pieces from the lives of a variety of people that we have known.

Chapter 2 takes you into self-analysis, so you can examine and measure how well you listen. After identifying problem areas, you will be introduced to solutions. Easy to follow techniques will help you replace bad habits with good ones.

Chapter 3, "Overcome Challenge Number One with Effective Listening," will show how the benefits of effective listening touch every area of your life. Your personal autonomy, productivity, and relationships will all be influenced by more effective listening.

Chapter 4 demonstrates that understanding the speaker's purpose and learning how to respond appropriately to the various purposes will save you time and increase the value of your business, family, friends, and associates. Chapter 5 explains you can reduce stress by becoming aware of when and where breakdowns in communication occur, and how to repair them. Difficult relationships can become positive ones as you apply the "RELATIONS" model presented in chapter 6. Furthermore, you will raise the esteem of those who communicate with you.

Emotions—their power, their effect on communication, and the know-how of their control is discussed in chapter 7. During the hundreds of conversations we have in a typical day, we try to influence people with our thinking. Chapter 8 demonstrates that the Language of Effective Listening is a dynamic persuasion tool, not a manipulation tool. Effective listening enables you to listen with integrity, yet persuasively, to the important people in your life.

Some researchers suggest that up to 90 percent of communication is nonverbal body language. Chapter 9 enables you to identify the meaning of nonverbal communication, so that you will build better communication with the five people you have identified.

Notetaking is a skill that effective listeners use to increase retention. Apply the lessons of chapter 10 on notetaking to increase retention and become more responsible in fulfilling obligations.

The concluding parable reviews and summarizes the action plan that, if followed, will bring you maximum benefit from using this book. On page 215 you will find a "tear out" return card to complete and mail for more information about a training session for your organization.

May God bless you as you pursue the benefits of the Language of Effective Listening!

O N E

A Tale of Two Managers

Barb and Bob worked in the same office, and both were considered by many to be on the fast track to the top of ABC Company. They were hard workers and about the same age, in their mid-thirties. The pair had made equally significant contributions to enhance the profits of their company. Furthermore, they had reputations as creative thinkers, incisive analysts, and excellent planners. Both had demonstrated superior academic abilities by graduating near the top of their college classes. Yet with all the similarities, a major difference emerged in their career paths. Barb eventually was promoted to the ranks of senior management. Bob wasn't.

Why did Barb stay on the fast track while Bob got derailed? In a word, Barb learned how to build strong supportive relationships on the job through what I call the "Language of Effective Listening." Bob, in contrast, failed to master this language, and his career suffered as a result.

To understand how this could happen, consider these brief but representative slices of life in ABC Company that feature first Bob and then Barb. In both cases, the "snapshots" of the two workers were taken when they were still in their thirties and considered candidates for top jobs in the company.

BOB'S TALE

When Bob arrived at his office one morning, his secretary told him that his boss, Sam, wanted to see him. But Bob was preoccupied by a near-accident during his commute to work. He brushed off his secretary and went immediately into his office. Just as he closed his door she managed to call out, "Sam did say he wanted to talk with you as soon as possible!"

However, Bob didn't pick up this final part of the message. Instead, without further questioning his secretary, he assumed that there wasn't any particular urgency to the matter. So he spent a few minutes tidying up his desk, taking care of several other things, and replaying in his mind the sequence of events that led up to the near-accident.

When Bob finally walked into Sam's office, about forty-five minutes later, he got the picture that his boss's message had been urgent.

"Where have you been?" shouted Sam, a volatile and impatient type. "You're always late! Look, I need that Smith report you've been working on—*now*!"

"I was in the office," Bob said. He folded his arms across his chest, crossed his legs, and shifted his body slightly to the side. He didn't like to be on the receiving end of this sort of criticism. He had the uncomfortable sense that Sam had pushed him into a kind of fortress and now was battering away verbally trying to wound him.

"If you were in your office, why didn't you come over here to see me?" Sam pressed. "Didn't you get my message?"

"Sure I got it, but. . . "

"But you didn't think it was that important? Look, Bob, your performance on this project could go a long way toward making your future in this company. You've been doing a pretty good job so far, so don't blow it. Now, be sure you get me that report before noon, okay?"

Bob left this meeting angry, upset, and a little frightened. The first person he released his emotions on was his secretary. "Why didn't you tell me Sam's message was so urgent?" he said through clenched teeth.

"I tried to," she responded, "but you were in such a hurry you closed your door before I could explain."

"Well, stop me next time and get the full message across. That's your job! Understand?"

His secretary nodded glumly, but this sort of confrontation with Bob had occurred too often for her to accept his criticism easily. In fact, this accusation pushed her over the edge. She turned in her resignation within days.

As for Sam, this recent encounter with Bob just confirmed a feeling that he had been developing. Bob didn't seem to operate gracefully under the pressures that burden those in responsible management positions.

BARB'S TALE

The same morning, Barb arrived at ABC Company at almost exactly the same time that Bob did. In fact, they rode up in the elevator together. Barb was feeling some pressure that day, too. When she dropped off her son at his kindergarten class, he had been feeling sick, and she was worried about him. The problem could be his usual car sickness, she thought, but then again, maybe he's coming down with the flu that is going around.

As she passed her secretary, she was mulling over a decision to call the school nurse and ask her to keep an eye on the boy. But her secretary interrupted her thought, "Sam wants to see you about the Jones project."

Barb acknowledged the message and kept walking toward her office. But then, she stopped and consciously "shifted gears" mentally. She realized she didn't have enough information to respond appropriately to this message, so she asked the secretary, "Did he say when he wants to see me?"

"First thing this morning."

"Okay, buzz his office and tell him I'll be right in," Barb said.

Then, she immediately went into her own office, called the school nurse, and took care of the problem with her son. She didn't feel she could delegate this important family concern, and she knew it would only take a minute or two to notify the nurse. Also, by instructing her secretary to call Sam and let him know she was coming, she was able to keep the boss calm and satisfy his impatience to make quick contact with her.

When Barb walked into Sam's office, about five minutes later, the first thing he said was, "I've got your report on the Jones project and it's not adequate. We can't lose this client, Barb, and I've been counting on you to come through for us. Success with this project could be a feather in your cap for your future at ABC. But if you blow this, it could really look bad. Tell me, did you really spend some quality time on this?"

"Sam, I know this project is very important," Barb replied calmly. "I've placed it at the top of my list of things to do. But remember, you've also given me three other projects that are 'top priority.' I'm convinced that I can do a good job on all of them, but I sense that at this point, I need your expertise and guidance to back me up."

"What can I do?" Sam asked, leaning toward her.

"First of all, let's agree on how we're going to juggle all these projects so that they all get finished successfully and on time," Barb replied, leaning slightly toward him. "Then, I'd like to go over exactly what changes you want on the Jones project report." At that, Barb pulled out a notepad so that she could jot down Sam's instructions and suggestions.

When Barb returned to her office, she decided she should also pass on a little constructive criticism to her secretary.

"Let me share something with you that you should know, because you're an important member of this team," Barb began confidentially. "Sam is a little nervous about some of the projects we're working on, and rightly so, because they're important to the profit picture of the company. He has put a lot of trust in you and me, and that's why we're working with some of the most significant clients this company has.

"So be sure when you give me a message from him, or from anyone else, for that matter, that I get all of it at once. Okay? In fact, I think it will be best to write down the main points and hand me the note as soon as you see me. You'll recall I had to ask you this morning *when* Sam wanted to see me. I should have that information without having to ask for it.

"I know you have a lot to think about, and believe me, I wouldn't give these responsibilities to anyone else. I've made it clear to Sam and the other management personnel how valuable you are, and that's one of the reasons you're so well paid. I personally appreciate how well you're supporting me under all this pressure."

Barb's secretary *didn't* quit her job; in fact, she stayed with Barb throughout her later rise in the ABC Company hierarchy. Also, Sam felt quite good about the meeting with Barb, especially her willingness to do her job cheerfully and diligently, even when she was operating under a lot of pressure. He was gratified by her apparent respect for him and his abilities.

A LESSON IN THE LANGUAGE OF EFFECTIVE LISTENING

These two scenarios could be interpreted several ways. Some might argue that Barb's primary strength was that she was better prepared emotionally to deal with the stresses of life. Others might say that she was more organized. Still others might contend that she was more mature, more confident, or simply a nicer person.

All these points may be true, but there is something even more significant. Barb was able to handle those challenging situations at work and, hence, move up in the organization, because she had learned to effectively and powerfully use the Language of Effective Listening. Bob, in contrast, seemed to know almost nothing about listening in this special language.

Specifically, Barb showed that she had learned these lessons about the Language of Effective Listening:

- She could avoid the temptation to allow outside "noises," preoccupations, or daydreams to intrude on her ability to listen. She was rightly concerned about her son's nausea at school. But she was able to address that problem and still focus on the message from her boss.
- Barb "filtered" the truth from the emotional factors. She showed she knew how to accept criticism from Sam as well as the attempts at threatening, bullying, or persuasion in his statements. In this way, she was able to gain a sense of perspective on his criticism, evaluate it, and respond constructively.
- Barb demonstrated the ability to establish a rapport with Sam, despite his initial hostile approach to her. Using appropriate words and body signals of the Language of Effective Listening, she gave him the impression that it would be worthwhile and pleasant for him to build an ongoing working relationship with her.
- She was also able to pass on some constructive criticism to her secretary about how to convey messages in the office. Far from feeling threatened, the secretary walked away from the discussion with a sense that Barb valued her work and professional ability.

In achieving this result, Barb had observed, among other things, the "five-to-one" rule. That is, she mentioned five positive points about the secretary (count them) to the one criticism she offered. By weighing her negative observation so heavily with affirmations, Barb ensured that the criticism would indeed be constructive and not destructive.

In contrast to Barb's fluency in the Language of Effective Listening, Bob's interactions with Sam and with his secretary reflected an almost total ignorance of appropriate, achievement-enhancing communication. He allowed outside matters to preoccupy him and prevent him from getting a key message from his secretary. He responded defensively both verbally and nonverbally to Sam's strong, negative opening statements, and he was never able to recover. Then, still smarting from the encounter with his boss, Bob bludgeoned his secretary with verbal abuse and drove her out of the company.

Both Barb and Bob had a great deal going for them in terms of intellect, academic background, and business savvy. But Bob's strengths never led to personal success because he didn't know how to listen to others effectively and speak to them in terms that would build rather than destroy bridges of understanding and friendship.

Much of our own success rests on the sense of self-esteem, trust, and confidence that we nurture in others. No matter what a person's intellectual ability or educational background, he will never achieve true success unless his boss, subordinates, and colleagues really want to work with him. The opportunities for achievement go to those whom others like and trust. To establish this kind of solid, working relationship and friendship with others, it is absolutely necessary to listen to them effectively. In short, it's essential to become fluent in the Language of Effective Listening.

T W O

Analyze Your Listening Habits

For if we would judge ourselves, we should not be judged.—St. Paul

Self-examination is a prerequisite to self-development! Ten years of experience at Effective Communication & Development, Inc., has led us to believe that self-examination, done constructively, is one of the most beneficial steps toward personal responsibility and fulfillment. People who constructively judge themselves are easier to work and live with. Associates, family, and friends have more confidence in a person who accepts responsibility for his or her own development.

You will be guided through five proven steps of profitable self-analysis. Each step builds upon the previous. Your success will be directly related to your motivation.

1. Determine who will be the recipients of your new skill development. Who will receive the benefit of your improved listening habits? Focus on these people during your self-development period.
2. Determine which of your listening habits are nonproductive.
3. Examine your behavior to determine how frequently you listen nonproductively.
4. Identify what productive habits will replace the nonproductive ones.

5. Commit yourself to practicing these positive skills on a regular basis, at least eight times a day for twenty-one days.

Personal change requires motivation. It is a great motivation to have in mind specific people with whom you would like to improve your relationship. In the space below jot down the initials of five people with whom you would like to improve your communication relationship. Choose people from your professional and personal life. I will improve my communication relationship with the following individuals:

_____   _____   _____   _____   _____

TEN MOST PRACTICED NONPRODUCTIVE LISTENING HABITS

Examine the list of nonproductive listening habits and ask yourself how often you practice these habits when listening to the five people you chose from your professional and personal life. Following the description of the ten bad habits is a checklist to help you examine your listening habits.[1] Then you can plan what you will change and determine how to do it.

Bad Listening Habit # 1: Lack of Interest in the Subject Matter

> *There are no uninteresting subjects. There are only uninterested people.—G.K. Chesterton*

Those with the widest interests are the most successful and interesting people and the best listeners. Poor listeners have a very limited list of interests, and they frequently limit their professional development and personal satisfaction. Becoming interested in the subjects that interest the people you speak with has at least three benefits.

You raise the self-esteem of the speaker by demonstrating interest in what he or she is saying. You will always win by raising the self-esteem of the speaker. Self-esteem is the number one prerequisite to personal productivity. If that person is important to you, listen to him or her. When you listen, you say, "You *are* important to me." What that person is saying is important to him or her, therefore, it is important for us to listen. Think of a recent time that you were especially affected by someone listening to you, or remember how you felt as a child when someone really listened.

Agape, one of several Koine Greek words for love, has the most profound meaning. *Agape* is doing for others what they need. It is a love of doing, not of feeling. By acting in the best interest of the speaker, your feelings will frequently change toward the speaker's subject matter. But even if your feelings don't change, you have helped the speaker, and yourself, by listening.

Studies show that the most successful individuals, whatever their field, across all occupational lines, are those with the largest vocabularies. The average educated adult in the United States has about 2,000 words in his or her vocabulary and uses 400 of those words in 80 percent of his or her conversation. The most successful people have a few hundred more words in their working vocabulary.

These people are more successful than the average adult because they have a wider selection of solutions to problems. They have more hooks to hang their ideas on. We think categorically and categories are defined by words. The larger the vocabulary, therefore, the greater the capacity for thought categories providing alternative means for identifying and resolving problems. Psycholinguists call the capacity for various solutions "requisite variety." The two most efficient means of building a vocabulary and gaining requisite variety are through reading and listening.

Figure 2.1. Effective listeners seek something of value from every speaker.

Finally, effective listeners realize that everyone is an expert in some area in which the rest of us are ignorant. Everyone has his or her own genius. The effective listener discovers and profits from the genius in others. Become a constructively selfish listener and recognize that you can gain something from what a person says at least 80 percent of the time. Listen for what is valuable to you. As Lyman Steil says, "Ask, 'What's in it for me?' and look for the Value Moment of Listening." Eighty percent of the time you will discover something of value.

Immediately after the workshop Mary took a limousine to the airport. Skeptical that she would gain anything from anyone who spoke to her, she particularly doubted that the elderly limousine driver might offer anything of value. After all, she was a well-placed executive and had more knowledge than most people. But she decided to ask the driver if she could sit up front and speak with him. She used all of the skills she had practiced in the workshop in an attempt to draw him out. She asked the appropriate questions in the correct manner and used her "power listening" skills to direct the conversation toward what was of value. He told his stories as she listened.

Ten days later my telephone rang, and Mary excitedly told me what she had learned from the driver. "But," she gushed, "I didn't call to tell you that we can learn something from almost everybody. You already know that. I had to call because a florist just came to my office with an arrangement of flowers from the limousine driver. And. . . " At this point her voice broke, and she had difficulty getting out what she wanted to say. "And. . . with the flowers came this note, 'Dear Mrs. B. thank you for giving me one of the most wonderful mornings of my life!' " Mary was learning the benefits of effective listening.

Months later Mary called again. The limousine driver left his previous job to become the chauffeur for the vice president of an electronics firm. This firm was interested in purchasing components from Mary's company. Would Mary be interested in meeting his boss?

After a week of meetings in Chicago I was very tired. I love working with the people in our training sessions and I always try to give 110 percent to make it an enjoyable and beneficial experience for everybody. When I got my boarding pass I requested an aisle seat with the middle seat to be left open. In the window seat was a man who seemed very unlike me. I was wearing a typical three-piece business suit. He was wearing jeans, a cowboy shirt, and boots, and he had very long hair. I was glad we were dressed so differently, because I assumed he would naturally find our dissimilar appearance sufficient reason to ignore me. He appeared to be asleep. Gratefully, I picked up my book and began to read. I planned to spend a few minutes reading and then sleep the rest of the trip.

I had hardly dipped into the text when he spoke. "I see you're reading my favorite book." With that comment he hooked my attention. I had to decide if I should excuse myself and politely tell him I was tired, that I was about ready to take a nap and possibly could chat with him later, or allow the conversation to continue. I knew never to feign attention. This could be an ideal time to get a good illustration for our workshops. Here was a man whom I had never met and in all probability would never see again. Would he be able to tell me something of value if I gave him my undivided attention?

Although I was tired, I decided to give it a try. Turning toward him, and preparing to give 100 percent attention, I responded to his statement in a manner that would encourage conversation. For three hours I listened to him talk about his sales business, his single's club, and his personal aspirations. He got a "kick" out of the fact that, although he barely graduated from college, he was probably making twice as much as I, a college professor. His estimation was way off. He was making five times as much as I. We both had a good laugh over it.

I was tired when the conversation began. By the end, I was completely exhausted. Worse yet, I had learned nothing of value for all my effort. I consoled myself as I walked down the ramp, at least it was good practice in listening when tired. Then I heard him call my name, "Art, wait a minute, I'd like to have your card."

I gave him a card and asked why he wanted it. He replied, "You really listened to me, and in response to something I said, you mentioned a charity in Brooklyn that you help support. I want to support that charity and will send you a check every month for the next twelve months." And, he did! We had not met before, nor have we had occasion to meet again. But the trust level rose so high in that encounter, he was willing to send money to a complete stranger.

A man left the opening workshop session determined to listen to his wife. She had refused to concede that they needed a new car. He came back to our second day of training to tell us that his wife had agreed that a car was necessary, and they had already begun their search. Why this sudden turnaround? He listened to her "arguments" of why a new "car was not necessary," and found that she was not opposed to buying a new car. She only wanted a chance to express her opinion, to share her view, to be heard!

Don't expect 100 percent payoff. The probability is high that you will lose more insights and opportunities by *not* listening attentively, compared to the few nonproductive conversations you may have to endure. Even when there is no immediate payoff, you are reaping three benefits: (1) you are raising self-esteem, (2) you are developing your listening skills, and (3) you are learning and broadening your interests and vocabulary.

Bad Listening Habit #2: Being So Critical of the Speaker's Presentation that You Miss the Message

Effective listeners recognize the speaker's unusual speech, diction, accent, dress, hair style, grammar, and any other idiosyncrasies, and get beyond them to gain the content of the message. Our attention is quickly diverted by speakers who look at the floor, speak in a monotone, play with objects, or wear unattractive or inappropriate clothes.

When Albert Einstein walked through the Princeton University campus to give a lecture, students noticed that he wore sneakers, high-water pants, and no socks. The bad listeners chuckled during the entire presentation and missed the message. Effective listeners got beyond his unique appearance and were enriched by the content of his speech. Generally, the value of what we listen to is in the content, not in the delivery.

The hero of the early television series, "I Led Three Lives," was a counterspy named Herb Philbrick. A few years before the series aired, Douglas Hyde, a leading member of the Communist party in Britain, was the news editor of the *London Daily Worker.* In 1948, after twenty years as a Communist, he renounced the Party and joined the Catholic church with his wife and children. After his political and religious conversion he wrote *Dedication and Leadership*. The chapter entitled "The Story of Jim" illustrates the importance of getting beyond the appearance and focusing on the message and the person.

Hyde ended a lecture by saying that the Communist party could take anyone willing to be trained and turn him into a leader. Jim approached Hyde. Jim was very short, extremely overweight, with a flabby white face, a cast in one eye, and a most distressing stutter. Here was the greatest challenge Hyde could imagine. The first step was to build self-confidence and the second, to give him something to be confident about. Hyde gave Jim something to believe in and began to train him.

After some time, Hyde told Jim that he was ready to tutor others. He trained Jim to become a leader and groomed him for success as a tutor. Next, Hyde forced Jim to become articulate by giving him knowledge others didn't have and insisting he express it to others. Jim's next stage of development was as a street-corner propagandist and agitator. Finally, he became a national leader of his trade union.

A listener deceived by her slow speech may underestimate the acumen of one of the most intelligent women I have ever met in the corporate community. She suffers from Parkinson's disease and, although the motor movement of her tongue is slow, she has a legal mind with laser speed. Effective listeners get the content and avoid stumbling over delivery errors. How often are valuable insights missed because the listener judges the person or the delivery, and not the content of the message?

Bad Listening Habit #3: Getting Overstimulated and Interrupting the Speaker

How often have you drawn a premature conclusion and inter-rupted the speaker either inwardly or outwardly, and then missed his or her point? Ultimately you realized the speaker was consistent and you were wrong. Effective listeners "hold their fire" until they have heard the complete message.

Figure 2.2. Effective listeners wait until the speaker is through, pause, think, and then respond.

Figure 2.3. Effective listeners get the point.

You don't like to be interrupted when you are talking. You want the listener to wait until you are finished, think about what was said, and then respond. Instead of interrupting and fighting for "air space," you need to hold your fire until the speaker is through. It's just as rude to step on someone else's ideas as it is to step on his or her toes.

Bad Listening Habit #4: Focusing on the Details and Missing the Point

Poor listeners, like "Dragnet's" Sergeant Friday, listen only for the facts. If you focus solely on details, you may miss the point. Effective listeners identify the *concept*. The concept is like the hub of a wheel; the facts are the spokes. If the facts are not connected to the concept when the pressure of time bears upon the wheel, the wheel becomes unbalanced and throws off the spokes. The facts are lost. We remember what we understand. How often have you been taken literally and misunderstood?

"Look out!" someone yelled to the man standing on the subway platform. He immediately stuck out his head over the track to look, and was hit by the passing train.

After four years of college, the graduate decided on a career as a chicken farmer. He bought some land and some chickens. He planted row upon row of chickens with their heads deep in the fertile soil. They all died the next day. He wrote his alma mater, described the situation, and requested help. The return letter said, "We can't help you without a soil sample."

Bad Listening Habit #5: Forcing Everything into a Preconceived Outline

Poor listeners rarely take notes. If they do, they force them into a preconceived outline, imposing their own organizational pattern on the speaker. Effective listeners identify the speaker's outline and follow it while taking notes or thinking through the speaker's message.

Overcoming personal preconceptions helps you hear things as they are, not as you want them to be. Poor listeners often mentally edit remarks they don't like or distort meanings to avoid coming to grips with viewpoints they resent.

Bad Listening Habit #6: Demonstrating an Inactive Body State

Poor listeners habitually display an inactive body state. Effective listeners recognize that their physical stance influences their ability to concentrate. They use the RELATIONS model (discussed in chapter 6). A sloppy posture frequently denotes an unconcerned attitude. When you adopt a positive physical stance you automatically become more attentive. When was the last time you pretended to listen but your mind was actually miles away? If you pretend, people will see through you.

While daydreaming in the second grade, I was startled into the present by the teacher's voice, "Now turn in your papers, class." What had she asked us to write on the paper? My mind raced. I looked at the paper of the girl sitting next to me—hers was done and ready to be turned in. Hurriedly I copied what she had written. "Whew!" I breathed a sigh of relief. You can imagine my surprise when, a few minutes later, the teacher asked, "Why are there two papers for Linda and none for Arthur?" The teacher had instructed us to put our name, address, and date at the top of the page. I had copied the name and address of the girl sitting next to me.

Don't fake attention. If you cannot give your full attention, postpone the important conversation.

Bad Listening Habit #7: Tolerating or Even Creating Interfering Distractions

The specific area in the room within the speaker's view that attracts his attention and where the speaker is least distracted is called the "cone of attraction."[2] Those who stand or sit outside this cone are less likely to receive the full attention of the speaker and more likely to be distracted. The closer people sit to each other, the more likely they are to listen carefully.

Figure 2.4. Effective listeners get rid of distractions.

Poor listeners believe that circumstances control their lives. Effective listeners take control by eliminating as many distractions as possible or by listening through distractions they cannot remove. How often do you allow the telephone to interrupt a conversation? When a conversation is interrupted, the listener forgets the last few seconds of what was said even though he or she is trying to concentrate on the conversation.

Recognize and eliminate distracters. At home people leave the television on while talking at the dinner table. At work people turn their desks to see what is happening in the hallway or outer offices. At parties people try to greet everyone while talking to a long-lost friend.

Individuals who believe they have some control over their circumstances are the happiest people. We can probably do more to create a listening environment free of detrimental distractions. Family members may find it helpful to set aside special times for undistracted conversation. Make it a rule not to conduct telephone conversations at mealtime. If you're right-handed, place the telephone on your left side. Remove distracting pictures and arrange your desk to eliminate visual distractions. Communication is always better when we put others at ease and establish an agreeable atmosphere.

Bad Listening Habit #8: Tuning Out Difficult Material

Poor listeners tune out difficult material. Good listeners work on building their vocabulary and exercising their minds. They listen to people, discussions, and presentations that will expand their vocabulary. The average television program is written for a sixth grade vocabulary. Effective listeners understand this and, although they enjoy this level of material, on

Figure 2.5. Effective listeners strengthen their minds by listening to difficult and different vocabulary and concepts.

occasion, they seek out articulate programs such as "Nova" and "Meet the Press." Whatever your political affiliation, William Buckley will challenge you to learn new vocabulary. Individuals who remain active and grow mentally gain IQ points in their older years. Your verbal intelligence will increase and you'll become a more productive and valuable person to yourself, to your company, and to your family and friends, even after retirement.

> *The mind, once expanded to the dimension of*
> *larger ideas, never returns to its original size.—*
> *Oliver Wendell Holmes*

Our ears need practice for more difficult listening situations. In addition to the challenge of listening for new words and thoughts, use reading as a vocabulary builder. Look up words you don't know. You don't have to understand all of the words in a sentence to recognize its meaning. Too often we "bail out" of the conversation when with a little effort we could understand what is being said. Here are simple, familiar thoughts expressed in unfamiliar terminology. How many "obfuscations of celebrated oracular utterances" can you figure out?

1. Scintillate, scintillate, asteroid minific.
2. Members of an avian species of identical plumage congregate.
3. Surveillance should precede saltation.
4. Pulchritude possesses a solely cutaneous profundity.
5. It is fruitless to become lachrymose over precipitately departed lacteal fluid.
6. Freedom from encrustations of grime is contiguous to rectitude.
7. Eschew the implement of correction and vitiate the scion.

8. It is fruitless to attempt to indoctrinate a superannuated canine with innovative maneuvers.
9. The temperature of aqueous content of an unremittingly ogled saucepan does not reach 212 degrees Fahrenheit.
10. All articles that coruscate with resplendence are not truly auriferous.

Answers: 1. Twinkle, twinkle little star. 2. Birds of a feather flock together. 3. Look before you leap. 4. Beauty is only skin deep. 5. Don't cry over spilled milk. 6. Cleanliness is next to godliness. 7. Spare the rod and spoil the child. 8. You can't teach an old dog new tricks. 9. A watched pot never boils. 10. All that glitters is not gold.

Bad Listening Habit #9: Allowing Your Emotions to Be Triggered to the Point Where the Message is Blocked

Emotions are wonderful and important. They bring color, meaning, and purpose to our lives. Emotionally laden words give great satisfaction or can arouse personal antagonism. Anyone who knows more about what touches our emotions than we do is in a position to control us. Millions of dollars are spent every year to control us through our emotions. When emotions go up, rationality goes down.

In some of our workshops we used tape recordings of very emotional topics, such as "Right To Life," versus "Freedom of Choice." Different voices present the "pro" and the "con" sides of the issues, but the same statistics are used by both presenters. After listening to the tapes, the participants are asked ten questions.

Following the presentation of one side of the argument, a man came forward and requested a copy of the tape so he could disprove the statistics that were presented. I told him that both sides of the tape contained the same statistics; it was the nonverbal communication, not the data, that made the difference. He was so emotionally aroused he could not hear me! We cannot win an argument, much less gain a hearing, without listening to the other side. Emotional control makes hearing possible.

On a long drive I tuned my car radio to a talk show that held views opposed to mine. Seconds after listening to the discussion, I sensed the bias in the speaker and found my emotions going through the roof of the car. But I forced myself to listen, I gained emotional control, and I even learned something. "Those" people knew something that I didn't know. If we identify what touches our emotions and practice control, we can gain emotional control.

Bad Listening Habit #10: Wasting the Advantage of Thought Speed by Daydreaming

Good listeners take advantage of the fact that they think seven to ten times faster than anyone can talk. They use this advantage of thought speed to process the message—to evaluate, to review, to anticipate, and to summarize the message the speaker is sending. They look for the purpose and for key words and concepts. Good listeners discern the overt and subliminal outline of the message. They recognize the significance of the emotional content and attitude, as well as the conceptual and verbal content. They are aware that more than 700,000 nonverbal cues are sent to them. By concentrating and exercising certain techniques, they learn more about what the speaker is saying than the speaker often intended to convey. Compressed speech through tape players with Variable Speech Control demonstrates that the average adult can listen to 282 words per minute with no loss in comprehension, yet the average person speaks about 150 words per minute. Your greater thought speed enables you to process and evaluate.

SELF-ASSESSMENT

*The life which is unexamined is not
worth living.—Plato*

Take a moment to examine yourself according to the criteria explained above. Think of the five people you want to improve your relationship with during the next thirty days. Indicate which idea most closely describes your listening habits: Almost Always (A.A.), Usually (Usu.), Sometimes (St.), Seldom (Se.), or Almost Never (A.N.). (See Table 2.1.)

The national average for this self-examination is sixty-two. Your associates and friends may or may not agree with you. Their perception may be different from yours. One way to compare your perception with their perception of your listening behavior is to use the confidential, positively oriented, computerized listening inventory. (The computerized listening inventory is available from Effective Communication & Development, Inc. See Figure 11.1.)

In the first column below, list the initials of the five people with whom you want to enhance your communication. In the second column, write the habit you want to eliminate and in the third column, write the number of the habit.

Person	Habit (negative statement)	Habit
a.		
b.		
c.		
d.		
e.		

LISTENING HABIT	ALMOST ALWAYS	USUALLY	SOME-TIMES	SELDOM	ALMOST NEVER	INITIALS
1. Uninterested in the subject matter.						
2. Being critical of speaker.						
3. Interrupting the speaker.						
4. Focusing only on the details and missing the point.						
5. Not synchronizing with the speaker.						
6. Adopting an inactive body state such as slouching, etc.						
7. Allowing interfering distractions.						
8. Avoiding unfamiliar or difficult material.						
9. Allowing emotions to be triggered.						
10. Wasting the advantage of thought speed (daydreaming).						
TOTAL SCORE						

SCORE KEY: Almost Always/2   Usually/4   Sometimes/6   Seldom/8   Almost Never/10

Table 2.1.   Listening habit

TURN YOUR TRIALS INTO TRIUMPHS

The receivers' coach for the New York Giants football team was experiencing one of the worst seasons in the team's history. On an average, professional football coaches last less than three years with a team. At the end of this season, all the offensive coaches were fired. For Ted Plumb, it was one of the worst years of his life.

Ted was hired by another club, where, driven by his character and intelligence, he applied what he had learned with the Giants. This enabled him to help the Chicago Bears win the Super Bowl. He said that he took one step backward in order to take two steps forward. He learned from his mistakes. Mistakes are stepping stones to success if we are willing to learn from them. Some Japanese companies require their employees to make a certain number of mistakes each year. Only by making mistakes, the companies reason, will employees learn new things and become better.

Count the cost! Is it worth the effort to learn a new habit that will build better relationships, even if you fail in some of your attempts to improve?

Turn your trials into triumphs! Compare the list of skills below with the list of nonproductive listening habits. Those negative habits are restated below as positive skills. Circle the skills below that correspond to the habits you plan to change.

LISTENING SKILLS

1. Listen for something of value in what the person is saying. Raise his or her self-esteem.
2. Judge the content of the message, not the deliverer or the delivery of the message.

3. Use "active silence." Remain silent, but listen until the person is finished speaking. Think about what was said, pause, and then respond.
4. Get past the details to the main point.
5. Synchronize with the speaker's verbal and nonverbal communication.
6. Adopt an active body state. Lean toward the speaker in an alert body position.
7. Control or eliminate distractions.
8. Concentrate on unfamiliar material and stretch your mind.
9. Practice emotional control.
10. Take advantage of thought speed. Put on your E.A.R.S. (Evaluate, Anticipate, Review, and Summarize) while the person is talking. Listen for key words and be aware of nonverbal messages.

Now write the initials of the same five people with whom you will build more effective communication. In the second column list the listening skills that you want to develop with each person. Restate them in your own words. Bad habit numbers and positive skill (good habit) numbers should correspond.

	Person (same initials)	Habit (positive statement)	Skill #
a.	_____	_____	_____
b.	_____	_____	_____
c.	_____	_____	_____
d.	_____	_____	_____
e.	_____	_____	_____

MAKE THE COMMITMENT AND SIGN YOUR CONTRACT

Signify that you are making the commitment to improve your communication relationship with the five people you have named by signing your name. Make the commitment now.

Name: _____ Date: _____

VISUALIZE YOUR SUCCESS NOW

During my senior year at U.C.L.A. I had the privilege of teaching students in the psychology clinic how to improve their reading skills. Junior and senior high school students from around the country increased their reading level by two or three years in just eight weeks of training. This tremendous growth was made possible by a unique program that incorporated as many senses as possible in the learning process. That experience and other studies demonstrate that you are more likely to succeed in learning a new positive skill if you write out your actions, listen to yourself say them, relax, and watch yourself perform those actions.

The thought process that enables you to target your actions is further imprinted on your brain when you write it out. You will do what you think about. If you can visualize yourself listening to people, you will have taken another giant stride toward accomplishing your goal. Usually, if you can vividly imagine it, you can do it. This is what Denis Waitley and others call "scripting."

Visualize your success to help make it a reality. In order to begin the visualization process, you must be able to relax. As you guide yourself through this exercise, you will learn how to control yourself in a new way. This visualization exercise is often more effective than physically listening to people. Prepare for the visualization exercise by asking yourself:

Who will I listen to?
What will that person look and sound like?
Which listening skills will I use?
Where will I be listening to that person?
When will this take place?
How do I want to feel when listening to this person?

The following suggestions will help make your visualization experience more successful.

Choose a time and a place where you will not be interrupted.

Play soft music on the radio or stereo. Classical music at about sixty beats per minute is ideal because sixty beats per minute is about the average heart rate in a relaxed mode.

Listen to a recording of your own voice to help you relax. The more relaxed you are, the more effective the exercise.

Place your feet on the floor, sit up in your chair, close your eyes, and slowly inhale and exhale ten times. With each exhale, feel your body relax from the top of your head to the tip of your toes. When you feel relaxed, look for the person in your imagination and try to visualize his or her face. Attempt to hear the voice of the person you are imaging and try to create the type of feeling you would like to have when listening to him or her. Imagine yourself raising the person's self-esteem by using effective listening skills. Using the listening skills you selected, change the pictures, the sounds, and the feelings until they are just what you want. Then, imagine the ongoing conversation for a couple of minutes and draw it to an appropriate close.

Practice this exercise during the next thirty days and reap the rewards!

T H R E E

Overcome Challenge Number One with Effective Listening

Communication is everything. Task performance—and life for that matter—are simply by-products of communication patterns.—
Tom Peters

American businesses face the challenges of world competition and a shrinking dollar. Ecological and ethical issues cram our newscasts. Our problems are monumental. In his book, *Celebration of Life,* the sociobiologist Rene Dubos, looks behind the growing dilemma in our world. "The most distressing aspect of the modern world is not the gravity of its problem. There have been worse problems in the past. It is the dampening of the human spirit that causes many people, especially in countries of Western Civilization to lose their pride in being human and to doubt that we will be able to cope with our problems and those of the future."[1] The greatest challenge we face today is our need to recover hope.

Loss of hope is often manifest as depression. "Depression, which is often related to low self-esteem, costs the United States of America five billion dollars a year in direct drug and hospital costs."[2] We do not know the indirect cost to our country in terms of broken families, alcoholism, drug addiction, and poor business. All productivity is related to self-esteem. Consequently, the number one challenge is to restore hope.

When you esteem yourself you are more likely to do a better job. Untapped creative power is unleashed. You are open to positive change and welcome the challenge of new opportunities. You are more open to others, more honest in your dealings, and more likely to be supportive of your company, community, country, faith, and home. Self-esteem lies at the root of moral and ethical sensitivity. To esteem yourself is to lay the groundwork for more successful, interpersonal relationships. Furthermore, if you have self-esteem, you are less likely to develop a chemical addiction. When you esteem yourself you build a strong sense of family, are more involved in social and political activities, and are generous to the less fortunate.[3]

As an added bonus, when you place appropriate value on yourself, those around you are infected with the same positive virus. What you think of yourself is more important than what others think of you. What you think of yourself will be reflected back to you in the attitudes and actions of those with whom you work and live.

RAISE SELF-ESTEEM THROUGH EFFECTIVE LISTENING

Self-esteem is related to communication. A short route to self-esteem is to esteem others; therefore, to receive respect, you must show respect. Remember the old proverb "You reap what you sow"? Listen! Listen to your associates, colleagues, friends and loved ones.

What people say is important to them, even if it isn't important to you. You can build their esteem and your own by learning effective listening habits. Listening is the foundation for all effective communication. When you listen to your colleagues and associates you give them hope because you esteem them.

To determine how you influence your associates, colleagues, family, and friends, take the self-assessment inventory. (See Table 3.1.)

How often do you listen in a manner that produces these results?

EFFECTIVE LISTENING BRINGS PROFESSIONAL AND ECONOMIC BENEFITS

Among students of at least average intelligence, the correlation between their ability to listen and their grades is higher than the correlation between their IQ and their grades. What is true in the academic community is true in the business world as well. *Individuals who have gone the furthest in their profession are, characteristically, better listeners. These achievers also have a wide range of interests as a result of their effective listening.*

The benefits of effective listening include greater productivity, increased understanding, and increased job potential and operating efficiency. Add to these benefits the reduction of wasted time and materials. Time saved translates into saved dollars, energy, and productivity. As an example, a major computer company taught its employees effective listening skills and took ten million dollars in business away from a competitor in just one city. If your company employs 100 people and each one raises his or her listening efficiency by 10 percent, you would make significant gains in productivity.

Research statistics identified why customers stopped buying from a company. Table 3.2 shows that 68 percent abandoned the supplier because of an employee's attitude of indifference toward a customer. Effectively listening goes a long way toward showing customers and clients an attitude of concern instead of indifference.

	ALMOST ALWAYS	USUALLY	SOME-TIMES	SELDOM	ALMOST NEVER	INITIALS
1. The speaker is glad to talk with you, even if you disagree on the validity or value of what he or she said.						
2. The speaker knows that you understand both the thoughts and feelings of what was said.						
3. You are glad to converse with the speaker even if you disagree with him or her.						
4. You know and convey to the speaker your understanding of his or her thoughts and feelings.						
5. Both you and the speaker have more energy now to devote to immediate tasks than before you listened.						
TOTAL SCORE						

SCORE KEY: Almost Always/2   Usually/4   Sometimes/6   Seldom/8   Almost Never/10

Table 3.1. Self-Assessment: Does your listening build self-esteem?

1%	Die
3%	Move Away
5%	Because of other friendships
9%	Because of competition
14%	Product Dissatisfaction
68%	Attitude of indifference toward a customer by an employee.

Table 3.2 Why customers quit

EFFECTIVE LISTENING IMPROVES MARRIAGE AND FAMILY LIFE

During the past ten years more than 90 percent of managers and professionals in effective listening workshops were more interested in improving communication at home than in their professional arena. Divorce statistics disguise the widespread desire to achieve harmonious, satisfying relationships at home. If effective communication increases productivity and satisfaction on a job that will end in retirement, just think what it could do for relationships you want to last a lifetime?

Effective listening helps you increase your knowledge and experience as you ask questions and really listen to the answers. Listening enables you to rapidly gain information that would otherwise take days, weeks, or years to learn if instead you read books, sit in front of a computer terminal, or watch television. You can build friendships, help others solve their problems, resolve disagreements, enhance cooperation, make better decisions, avoid conflicts, increase confidence, and enhance enjoyment.

Listening to others discuss their problems and viewpoints can reduce tension within a family and between friends. In marriage, the ability to negotiate differences is the greatest predictor of success. Effective negotiation requires effective listening. Of the four most frequently stated reasons for divorce, couples cited ineffective communication as the number one problem. The other three most frequently stated reasons are money problems, problems with the children, and sexual problems. All four reasons relate back to difficulties in communication.

The money problem did not spring primarily from lack of funds, but rather from not being able to communicate "how to spend what we have." Problems with children evolved from disagreements on how to deal with the children; also a communication problem. Similarly, most sexual problems result from communication difficulties. A sexual relationship involves communicating on many different levels; hence, ineffective communication will result in sexual dysfunction.

"Seeing yourself through your partner's eyes could work wonders," suggests Samuel Schreiner, Jr., in his article, "A Question that Can Save Marriages." Schreiner asks couples to ask themselves, "*What* is it like to be married to me?" As you answer this question you get your partner's mind-set and you see, hear, and feel as he or she would. You listen to yourself as you perceive your partner to listen. Schreiner cites incidents of dramatic change when a husband or wife listened to themselves and realized how he or she must seem to the other.[4]

EFFECTIVE LISTENING IS GOOD FOR YOUR HEALTH

To be human is to communicate—to talk, listen, and respond to other human beings. But this constant dialogue has a dramatic effect on our bodies, especially on the heart and blood vessels. In his pathbreaking work, Dr. James Lynch conclusively demonstrates for the first time how simple human dialogue dramatically affects the body's entire cardiovascular system. The familiar process of talking and listening to others has important consequences for health and well-being.

The "language of the heart," according to Dr. Lynch, is much more than a poetic metaphor for thoughts and feelings we cannot name; it is a medically established reality. By using new technology to continuously monitor blood pressure and other "vital signs," Dr. Lynch and his associates investigated the impact of human dialogue among sufferers of hypertension and migraines, as well as people with normal blood pressure.

The findings astonished subjects and researchers alike. The blood pressure of every subject rose when he or she spoke and went down when each listened. Even more intriguing, most of the subjects were completely oblivious of these dramatic changes. Dr. Lynch argues with the zeal of an evangelist that this "language of the heart" cries out to be heard; if ignored, unanswered, or misunderstood, it can produce terrible physical suffering, even premature death. (See Table 3.3.)

BLOOD PRESSURE LEVEL	MEN		WOMEN	
	AGE 35	AGE 65	AGE 35	AGE 65
140/90	3 years	2 years	2 years	1.5 years
160/95	6	4	4	3
180/100	8	5	5.5	4

Table 3.3. Years of life lost due to hypertension[5]

LISTENING WELL DOESN'T COME EASY

Eighty percent of all business communications must be repeated, and rarely is more than 20 percent of what top management says understood five levels below.[6] Few people realize how much of their life is spent listening and how poorly they do it. Even fewer understand how important listening can be economically and socially, in terms of self-fulfillment. Listening is the number one problem in managerial efficiency. The mortar and cement of business are its communication systems.

People in business are discovering that the spoken word rather than the written word is the fulcrum on which significant communication turns. The effectiveness of the spoken word hinges not so much on how people talk, but on how they listen. Poor listening skills are responsible for more breakdowns in communication and resultant loss in productivity than any other skill or management technique.

Your time is precious, yet frequently time is lost through ineffective communication and listening errors. You make plans for a dinner date tonight; your guests planned to come tomorrow. You thought your partner said Columbus, Ohio, not Columbus, Georgia, and you fly to the wrong city.

When Italian economist and sociologist Alfredo Pareto discovered that 80 percent of Italy's wealth was owned by 20 percent of the people, he established the 80/20 principle. Subsequent findings show that 80 percent of sales are engendered by 20 percent of the sales force, and 80 percent of profits come from 20 percent of a company's products. Even 80 percent of personal productivity arises from only 20 percent of one's skills.

By applying Pareto's 80/20 principle, Dr. Harold Smith of Brigham Young University demonstrated the importance of listening as a management tool. Smith asked 457 certified administrative managers, "Which of the many management skills are most important to success?" The twenty skills that appeared most frequently were identified and placed in random order. Then 250 certified administrative managers were asked to place the skills in order of importance. The top five skills were communication skills. Listening was ranked number one.[7]

According to the *Harvard Business Review,* the ability to communicate is the most promotable quality an executive, manager, salesperson, or anyone can possess. The University of Michigan Graduate School asked 1,158 newly promoted top executives which courses best prepared them for business leadership. Business communication was the most common response with 71.4 percent rating it as very important. Finance was the second highest with 64.7 percent.[8]

OLD HABITS DIE HARD

In our hurry-up society, where everything needs to be done yesterday, we think we don't have time to listen. We think about our own concerns or how we will respond to the person talking to us. As soon as the person is through speaking, we say what we want to say or, worse yet, we interrupt before the person is finished.

We could hear even before birth. Some researchers say we recognized our mother's voice in utero at six months. By the time we were born, we preferred female voices. Our eyesight was poor at birth, about 20/500 or "legally blind." As it rapidly developed, we began to imitate our mother's facial movements. We could detect the relationship between her mouth movements and the sounds she made.[9]

As children we were very attentive to what our environment said to us. Often we understood more about what our parents were saying to each other than our parents did. Listening was a survival skill.

By the time we entered first grade, we unconsciously concluded that it was not necessary to be attentive even when someone was speaking directly to us. This inattention became our listening style, a noncommunication skill that was maintained through school and into the business world. No one corrected us and rarely were good listening skills required or rewarded. It's no wonder the average adult listens below a 25 percent efficiency level. (See Figure 3.1.)

TO PROFIT FROM EFFECTIVE LISTENING YOU MUST INVEST

Internal and external stress factors prevent us from listening effectively. Past experience acts like a filter prejudicing us to the meaning the speaker is trying to convey. As senders (speakers) and receivers (listeners), our backgrounds, educations, presuppositions, prejudices, belief systems, and experiences provide mental filters through which we understand the words that we send and receive.

The unabridged English dictionary has 450,000 words, but regardless of education, the average person uses only 400 words in 80 percent of his or her spoken vocabulary.[10] You might think that 80 percent of our communication problem would be solved if we understood the primary meaning of those 400 words. The difficulty is that those basic 400 words have 14,500 different meanings. To further cloud the issue, language is changing so rapidly that one thousand new meanings are added to familiar vocabulary each year. With so many meanings for relatively few words, it is no wonder that the message we heard was not the message sent. We dare not assume that because we use the same word in a conversation we mean the same thing. The word prejudice means to *prejudge*. We are all prejudiced.

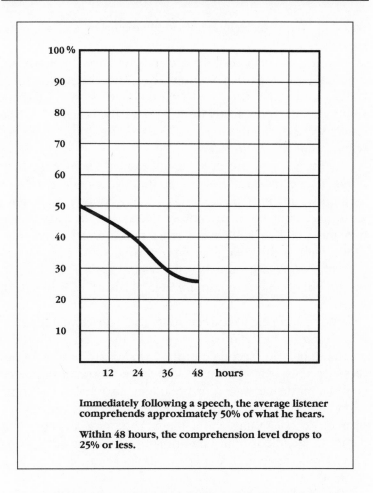

Figure 3.1. Average listening efficiency is poor.

One of the first principles in becoming a more effective listener is to realize that we are prejudiced. Our prejudices may lead us to make invalid assumptions about what people are saying. Assumptions are based on faith. Faith, in turn, is based upon our experience or on the experience of someone we trust.

We are alike in that we are all prejudiced, but we are different in our particular prejudices. The closer we are in background, education, experience, belief system, and assumptions, the more likely we will understand each other. The closer we are genetically to the speaker, the more likely we will communicate effectively.

Identical twins are able to understand each other with minimal external cues. Even when they are separated at birth and grow up at opposite ends of the country, they tend to develop the same prejudices, likes, and dislikes. When they meet in their adult years, twins find it easier to communicate with each other than with anyone else. They like to be with people who are like them because it is easier and more comfortable to communicate. "Birds of a feather flock together."

The first hurdle to leap en route to better communication is recognizing that you have prejudices that lead you to false assumptions. The second hurdle is to identify those prejudices. Accents, hair styles, and clothes predispose or prejudice you in a particular way. Your prejudgments need not become a roadblock to communication. Once you identify your biases plan to do something about them. Your best strategy is to withhold judgment until you are sure of the message being sent. Don't assume the person understands or that you understand.

Eugene Raudsepp of Princeton Creative Research tells the story of a zoologist walking down a busy city street with a friend amid honking horns and screeching tires. He says to his friend, "Listen to that cricket!" The friend looks at him with astonishment. "You hear a cricket in the middle of all this noise?" The zoologist takes out a coin and flips it into the air. As the coin clinks to the sidewalk a dozen heads turn in response. The zoologist says quietly, "We hear what we listen for."[11]

We are prone to practice Selectivity. We listen with "Selective Exposure," listening primarily to opinions that agree with our own. We evaluate on the basis of Selective Interpretation, interpreting messages the way we want to understand them, often adapting them to our own preconceptions. With Selective Memory we internalize the messages, remembering material that supports our own viewpoints and forgetting material that does not. Assigning meaning to a term is an internal process; meaning comes from inside us.

Many internal "noises" prevent us from hearing let alone understanding what a person says. Physically, we may be tired, hungry, have a cold, or be uncomfortable. The environment may be too hot or too cold. Our minds may be distracted by an argument we had a few minutes earlier, or we may be working on an unresolved problem. Fearfulness may cause our minds to become closed. Listener anxiety and ego involvement tend to decrease listener comprehension.[12] Objectivity tends to increase listener comprehension. "A person's mind is like a parachute; unless it is open, it doesn't function."

How many times have you tried to listen while you were doing something else? How well can you listen while you're trying to review a report or watch for an associate who will arrive anytime. Job stress or concern with what you are going to say distracts you from effectively listening to the speaker. The average attention span of the adult brain is twelve seconds.

Noises that are external to the speaker and listener may also be distracting. A running motor, a noisy air conditioner, other voices, and the number one distracter, the telephone, all affect effective communication. When any noise interrupts a conversation, the last few seconds of the conversation are lost unless they are reiterated. After an interruption, both parties need a moment to become reoriented and reestablish communication.

In addition to the internal and external noises between the sender and the receiver, sometimes the message itself is "noisy." Most messages have both denotative and connotative meanings; for example, consider the images conjured by the words "burnt dead cow" compared with "broiled steak."

Messages have latent as well as literal meanings. You send as clear a message with your tone of voice as you do with your words. A message as simple as "Look who's here!" can be laden with sarcasm, irony, or joy. Your voice's tone, pitch, volume, and modulation are the most powerful communicators of what you think and feel. Messages, like words, have different meanings in context. Subconscious and emotional needs may influence a message. What a person says may not be what he means. A complaint about his work may really mean that he's not getting along at home.

As communicators, our job is to determine what the speaker means by what he or she says. When you understand the internal noise filters, you will improve your understanding of what others are really saying. Even the most important people in your life will use words differently than you do, and you need to hear over this internal noise. Words have no meaning—people have meaning. Look for a common understanding. The word "communication" comes from the Latin root, *communis,* which means to have in common.[13] Effective communication is the ability to have a common understanding of the feelings and concepts being discussed.

LISTENING IS THE MOST FREQUENTLY USED COMMUNICATION SKILL

Eighty percent of our day is spent communicating. We are communicating beings. About half of our communication time is spent listening. Executives spend about 63 percent of their communication time listening.[14] In 1981, Dr. Larry Barker showed how our total communication time is divided into various activities. (See Table 3.4.)

Barker also showed that 21 percent of listening time is spent listening to mass communication such as the radio, television, or recorded music.[15] Before the advent of electronic media this time was used to interact with family members. The average father spends less than five minutes per week in quality communication time with a son or daughter, and no more than fifteen minutes per week with his wife. The statistics for mothers and wives are almost the same.

TRAINING IN THIS VITAL AREA HAS BEEN NEGLECTED

From the ancient philosophers to the present time, the primary emphasis in communication training has been on writing and speaking. Close to 200 billion dollars is spent every year on education in the United States, but almost no money is spent on listening training. Yet 57 percent of a grammar school student's time is spent in a listening mode; 53 percent of a high school student's time is spent in a listening mode; and 69

ACTIVITY	PERCENT OF TIME
Writing	14
Reading	17
Speaking	16
Listening	53

Table 3.4. How you use communication time

percent of a college student's time is spent in a listening mode.[16] More than 50 percent of managers' and supervisors' work time is spent listening. Eighty five percent of our Fortune 500 companies have listening training programs on tape, but less than 15 percent actively use them. (See Figure 3.2.)

If you want to be trained in the vital area of communication, you will have to train yourself. Taking responsibility for your own communication training is healthy and gratifying. A study conducted by the University of California revealed that the happiest and best adjusted adults were those who took responsibility for themselves.[17]

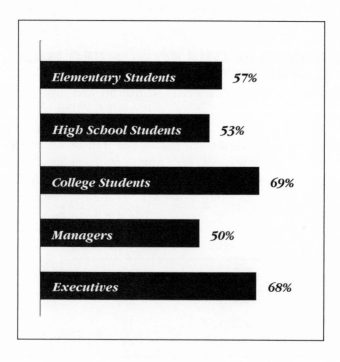

Figure 3.2. Average percentage of time spent in listening mode.

When asked, "Who is more responsible for effective communication, the speaker or the listener?" most workshop participants respond that the speaker is more responsible. The speaker chooses the subject, the context, and other variables. The listener, it is assumed, is passive. Such an assumption is a critical mistake. In some cases the speaker has something of value to say but communicates poorly. If the listener allows the speaker to have all the responsibility for communication, the listener loses out. Who robs the listener of vital information, the speaker with poor communication patterns or the listener who refuses to clarify the message?

ACCEPT THE 51 PERCENT RESPONSIBILITY CHALLENGE[18]

Accept the challenge to be responsible for understanding at least 51 percent of the communication in your life, whether you are the listener or the speaker. You'll be glad you did. As Dr. Lyman Steil says, "Don't buy it, just try it. If it doesn't work, let us know." If you accept the challenge, this book will enable you to profit from effective listening.

OBJECTIVES DETERMINE OUTCOMES

"If you don't know where you're going, you may end up somewhere else," said Yogi Berra when he was with the New York Yankees. We might say, "If you don't know where you are going, any road will get you there."

Florence Chadwick wanted to be the first woman to swim the channel between Catalina Island and the coast of California. She had already swum across the English Channel in both directions. The Fourth of July event would be historic. Unusually cold and foggy conditions, and shark-infested water made the swim more difficult. Riflemen sat on the bow of the two boats to escort her and shoot any sharks that came too close. She swam more than sixteen hours. Her mother and brother, who were in one of the boats, encouraged her to continue. Only a half-mile from shore she dragged herself out of the water. With television cameras focused on her, she answered the questions, "Why did you stop so close to your goal? Was the water too cold? Were you afraid of the sharks or too tired?"

"No," she responded. She explained that she could not see the shore through the fog. Swimming for hours without seeing the shore is very difficult. Before long this great lady attempted the swim again. This time she broke the men's record in the process. Her experience illustrates Aristotle's maxim, "We stand a greater chance of hitting the target if we can see it."

Without objectives we are like the man who went up to the airline ticket counter and asked for a ticket. "What is your destination?" the agent inquired. "Oh, anywhere will do," the man responded. If you don't know where you are going, you might end up where you don't want to be. We all must establish goals that are worthy of us as human beings!

In *Man's Search for Meaning,* Viktor E. Frankl described his three years at Auschwitz and other Nazi prisons. Some of the men in the camps simply willed themselves to die. Others actually grew in character. Frankl emphasizes in his therapy that a sufficient reason *why* you need to accomplish or reach a goal will always produce the means as to *how* you can do it!

Survivors in the prison camp were willing to give up immediate satisfaction, even in a small way, in order to reach a future goal. A crust of stale bread might alleviate immediate hunger pangs but provide less nourishment than the rancid soup, so the survivors chose the rancid soup, which did not alleviate hunger but provided some nourishment, in exchange for the more satisfying but less life-giving bread. The common denominator among the survivors was that each had a compelling reason to live. They wanted to survive the camp to tell the world about the living hell. Some were determined to be reunited with their families. Others felt they had to write a book or perform at a concert. They all had reasons for surviving that were bigger than themselves and greater than their circumstances.

Objectives determine outcomes. You accomplish what you aim for. A "servo" system in the brain called the reticular activating system directs you towards what you concentrate on. The system is automatic and works like a guided missile system.

OUR OBJECTIVES FOR YOU

The three general objectives are:

- To enable you to assess yourself and establish some specific goals.
- To give you insight into the cost of poor listening and the benefits of effective listening.
- To give you insight into the nature of listening as a crucial element in the communication process.

You can accomplish these objectives if you are motivated to take ownership of the learning process. You already identified five people in your professional or personal life with whom you would like to enhance your relationship. We guarantee that you will build mutual trust, understanding, and confidence with these people if you apply the principles that unfold to you.

As you read this book, think of the people with whom you would like to develop your relationship during the next thirty days and ask yourself how this material applies to your communication with them. Thinking about the people and principles, and planning how to apply these principles, will enable you to profit from this important communication skill.

F ● U R

Profit from Identifying the Speaker's Purpose

*One learns people through the heart, not the eyes
or the intellect.—Mark Twain*

Every conversation has a reason and every statement has a purpose. The impetus for the conversation may be conscious or unconscious, but the effective listener discerns the purpose of an individual's communication. The effective listener then gears his or her response toward that purpose. For example, any father of a teenager knows that the question, "Dad, is there gas in the car?" really means, "Can I borrow the car?"

Dr. Lyman Steil, founder of The International Listening Association and of Communication Development, Inc., suggests four purposes of communication.[1] The four purposes of communication are phatic, cathartic, informational, and persuasive. You need to be quick on your listening feet because the purpose of a conversation can change from moment to moment. As the purpose changes, the effective listener changes the way in which he or she responds. (See Figure 4.1.)

PHATIC COMMUNICATION

The first and most frequently used purpose of communication is small talk or *phatic* communication. Small talk is often regarded as trivial or even a waste of time, but it is the kind of communication that builds binding relationships. Casual chit-chat, "shooting the bull," and "chewing the fat" is important

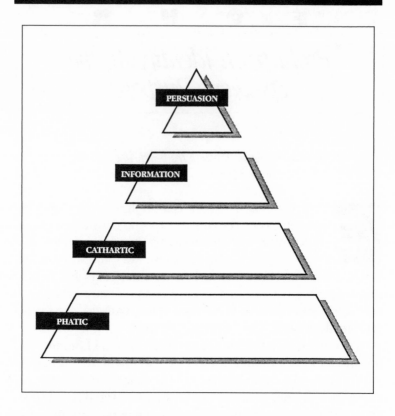

Figure 4.1. The four purposes of communication.

and requires a particular listening attitude and behavior. Phatic communication not only helps to develop binding relationships, but also contributes to higher levels of communication purposes. Without phatic relationships, other forms of communication become difficult and sometimes ineffective. We all have heard comments such as:

> "We worked together on and off for six years, but I never got to know him."

"I find it very hard to talk to her."

"He's a cold fish. I respect his abilities but I'd rather not work with him."

"I can't seem to reach that guy. He never pays any attention to us unless he wants something."

In most work environments two extremes are present. At one end of the phatic continuum is what Dr. Steil calls the (W)acky (E)xcessive (S)mall (T)alker, Fred "Gotta Minute."[2] Whenever you see Fred, he asks, "Have you got a minute?" and he will take a few minutes to tell you about last night's mashed potatoes.

The other extreme is John "Gotta Go." He is the (E)xcessive (A)voider of (S)mall (T)alk.[3] No matter what you ask John, if it isn't directly related to his business goals, he doesn't have time to answer. John does not develop binding relationships with people around him. His wife gives birth to twin girls and when you ask him about it, John's response is, "Everything's fine—gotta go." His brother is promoted to president of a major corporation. You mention this to him and he says, "That's right—gotta go." He wins the lottery and takes a trip around the world. You see him upon his return and ask him about it and he responds, "Good trip—gotta go." Nothing will bring John to discuss his feelings about events in his life.

John and Fred are as far apart in behavior and in understanding each other as the east is from the west. Fred "Gotta Minute" is always late finishing his reports, late coming to meetings, and late fulfilling his formal responsibilities. On the other hand, John "Gotta Go" is always on time with his reports, on time for meetings, and dependable in fulfilling responsibilities.

John is highly structured and goal oriented. However, no one really gets to know him and he doesn't know anybody. He is not close to his co-workers. His responses lack a certain amount of loyalty. On the other hand, Fred has a real team spirit. When the chips are down and you face a critical situation, John will ignore it because it is inconvenient, but Fred will stay up all night and work on a problem if it helps the team.

The most effective communicators are on the continuum somewhere between chatty Fred and all-business John. Small talk serves a purpose in the business community. Through casual chitchat we learn to recognize the prejudices of our co-workers. "Chewing the fat" helps us understand people better. As others sense the growing understanding, they are encouraged in their attitudes toward their work. The "right dose" of small talk builds team spirit, binds relationships, and increases productivity.

A woman who attended a public workshop several years ago discovered the value of casual, informal conversation. She had been promoted to supervisor of a pool of typists. When she accepted the position, she thought she should get to know her co-workers. She arrived at work thirty minutes early, set out coffee and coffee cake, and tried to get to know the employees. Within six months of her promotion the productivity level of the typing pool went from number five to number one.

Her practice of arriving early for small talk and coffee continued until she overslept one morning after working late the night before. She rushed to the office, fearful that her people would be very disappointed because their coffee wasn't ready. Imagine the pleasant surprise when she discovered that one of the employees had done the job for her. That's teamwork. After some reflection, she decided that she was no longer a necessary participant. Suddenly she had gained an extra half-hour in the day.

For the next year and a half she skipped the thirty-minute coffee time. One day she attended a listening workshop and during the discussion about phatic communication her eyes lit up. Enthusiastically she shared with the instructor what she thought was the solution to an important problem she faced on her job. The productivity of her organization had dropped from number one to number five within six months of dropping the coffee time. With the importance of phatic communication newly underscored, she decided to give the early morning coffee time priority.

Many of the people who had been a part of her pool when she first became supervisor had moved to other positions. She did not really know the individuals who had replaced them in her organization, and she had lost touch with those with whom she had enjoyed good communication. Six months later, after rejoining the coffee klatch, she called the workshop instructor to report that her organization was back in the number one position.

A major corporation in the Midwest was determined to increase phatic communication among employees. They did it simply and effectively by increasing the size of the tables in the lunchroom. It would no longer be possible for only three people to sit together at lunch or coffee break. By necessity, people were brought together. Phatic communication grew, and team spirit and productivity increased.

When someone asks, "How are you?" that person is not interested in a forty-five minute dissertation about your lumbago. Yet, that simple question in phatic communication is a thread of communication being sent to you. Ignoring the comment means breaking the thread. Many threads build strong ropes. Misunderstandings, like flaws in a thread, may appear in the rope of a strong relationship, but a breakdown in communication is only a broken thread. Just as a broken thread is not a broken rope, a single breakdown in communication is not a broken relationship. When a relationship is hanging on by a thread the breakdown in communication is very dangerous.

Strong relationships build greater productivity as a listener learns to recognize when a person is engaging in phatic communication. You can be *nonjudgmental* even if you don't agree with the person. Recognize that the speaker is trying to build a relationship. You may not be interested in scuba diving or hunting or gourmet cooking, but withhold judgment at this stage. Try to understand the speaker's presuppositions, background, and experiences. The best and least expensive way to show respect is to listen and try to understand that person. Say to yourself, "I have two minutes, and I'm going to give that person my full attention and respect."

Even a brief encounter that fully focuses on the speaker raises self-esteem, which is the key to raising productivity. We need to build the self-esteem of our people, our family, and our friends. In this way, everyone becomes more productive. A rewarding cycle is engaged because fruitful productivity enhances self-esteem. High self-esteem frees a person to esteem others more highly.

How to Develop Phatic Communication

Everyone, during his or her career, works with a John or Jane "Gotta Go." We are frustrated in our attempts to get to know them. It can be accomplished by using these helpful hints.

- First, become aware of the person's interests. Then, you can briefly talk about those interests and begin to develop a phatic relationship. Observe his or her style of clothing, car, jewelry, and office accents. Are there any pictures, books, or magazines in the person's office? These are all conversational clues to help you engage the person momentarily.
- When is this person most likely to invest in phatic communication? Before work, during break time, during lunch, or after work?

- Where is this person most likely to invest in phatic communication? A planned meeting or even a chance meeting at an "off site" location may be best. Old habits die hard. If the person characteristically does not talk at work, it will be much easier to converse at another location.

Improving phatic communication at home can be more difficult than at work. You can successfully apply the three points above to family and friends as well as to professional colleagues. Make a breakfast date instead of a dinner date with your spouse, and go to a new restaurant. Make a date with each of your children individually to eat at a new location. Follow these suggestions and *listen*. Everybody needs and wants somebody to listen to them.

How to Limit Phatic Communication

We all know what it is like to try to get a Fred or Frieda "Gotta Minute" to stop talking. We don't want to be rude, but we don't want to waste time either.

- Recognize who the "Gotta Minutes" are and prepare yourself to limit the conversation.
- Listen intently for two minutes or whatever amount of time you determine is appropriate.
- Restate what "Gotta Minute" said in your own words so that he or she knows you understood the conversation. Then tell him or her that you must move on to another task. If "Gotta Minute" persists, give him or her an appointment for a later date. Set the time and place.

These principles almost always work to perfection. Both the esteem of the speaker and the valuable time of the listener are protected, and a relationship grows.

SELF-ASSESSMENT EXERCISE Do you have enough phatic communication with the important people in your personal and professional life? Do you need to limit phatic communication with the people in your professional or personal life? In the space below, write the initials of the most important people in your personal and professional life.

Professional Life: _____ _____ _____

Personal Life: _____ _____ _____

Now put a plus sign by the initials of those with whom you want to increase your phatic communication and a minus sign by those with whom you want to reduce your phatic communication. Think about when, where, and how you will do this.

CATHARSIS

> *An official who must listen to the pleas of his*
> *clients should listen patiently and without rancor,*
> *because a petitioner wants attention to what he*
> *says even more than the accomplishing of that for*
> *which he came.—Ptahhotep, Egyptian Pharaoh,*
> *1000 B.C.*

A second purpose of communication is *catharsis*. The word catharsis comes from the Latin word meaning "to cleanse." The terms we use when we speak of catharsis are expressive of the act—get it off your chest, purge, let off steam, release emotions, vent feelings, and dump your bucket. Catharsis is emotional. Be aware when emotions go up because rationality goes down.

Catharsis can be either positive or negative in content, but emotions are strong on this level. If a person does not express these feelings, he or she will interpret all communication sent toward him or her through the internal filter of the emotional experience. Both the purpose of catharsis and the way the effective listener responds are different from phatic communication.

A man who won the lottery attended one of our workshops. From the moment he walked into the room it was quite obvious that something was on his mind. He was not able to concentrate on the business at hand until he had shared the news of his winnings with the group. Others have come to our workshops distracted by a "near accident" on the way to the session or by other disquieting experiences. Until these issues "get out," the internal noise is so loud that it is hard to concentrate objectively on what anyone else is saying.

Studies have shown that when people are invited to go into catharsis or to dump their bucket, 4 percent will physically accost you. They will kick, hit, spit, or bite. Sixteen percent will psychologically assault you. "Keep your blankety-blank proboscis out of my business." Eighty percent will dump their bucket.

We have all been in a public place or a conveyance when a total stranger has dumped his or her bucket, or we have dumped our own. In such situations of anonymity people sometimes think, "I'll never see this person again so I have nothing to lose. I'll tell him or her what is bothering me."

As you listen to catharsis try to understand the *feelings* the person is expressing. The conceptual content is not nearly as important as the feelings. In order to understand the other person's inner frame of reference, try to empathize. Empathy involves hearing, seeing, and feeling the world through the other person's ears, eyes, and other senses. If you focus only on the actual words that are spoken, but fail to listen for the deeper feelings, you often miss what is really being said. Ask yourself, "What is he or she feeling?" "What do these words and the way they are spoken tell me about what he or she might be experiencing?"

We sometimes use words not to communicate but to hide and obscure what we are feeling. We may try to distract our listeners. On other occasions we try to communicate our feelings but fail to find words that do an adequate job. Effective listening gets behind the words in an attempt to understand the deeper and often unexpressed feelings and meanings.

The challenge in listening to catharsis is twofold. First, try to understand the speaker's feelings. Second, reflect back and let the speaker know that you do understand. Your responsibility in listening to catharsis is to understand and express empathy, not to solve the problem.

To understand and reflect the feelings, you need to get on the same wavelength with the person while controlling your own emotions. The goal is to "pace" or walk with the person and sense his or her emotions by putting yourself in the same physical position. Try to reflect the speaker's physical position and gestures without giving the impression that you're mimicking him or her. If you're sincere about this, you begin to take on some of the physical characteristics of the person. This will enhance your ability to understand the person's emotions and to reflect them back in an understandable manner.

The speaker wants *empathy,* not necessarily the solution to the problem. Communicate empathy by reflecting what the person is feeling. Impatience, anger, or irrelevant cheerfulness during cathartic venting could be disastrous to a relationship. Catharsis requires a caring, empathic, and nonjudgmental listener. After you have identified with the person, understood, and reflected back his or her feelings, sometimes you can lead the speaker to a more objective state.

If a person never goes through catharsis, the emotional problem becomes a prejudiced filter through which everything else is seen, felt, and heard as long as the hurt or other feeling is there. Cathartic fulfillment is necessary for optimal success at all other levels of communication. Effective listeners are open to give and receive catharsis.

For whom should you provide catharsis? Almost everyone needs this type of communication to relieve tension. To whom can you safely let off steam? Of the individuals with whom you have phatic communication, you will find someone trustworthy and suitable to receive your catharsis.

Exercise caution in choosing the person to assist you in catharsis. Many careers have been ruined when a professional let off steam to the wrong individual and was misinterpreted. If you dump on the wrong desk, you're in trouble.

The best people to share catharsis with are those whom you have phatic communication with and know you can trust. In phatic communication, cautiously share significant tidbits and learn who you can trust. Trust grows slowly and mutually. People who share feelings with you are often expressing trust in you. Even angry communication is an expression of trust because it is revealing feelings to you.

How to Develop Cathartic Communication

If someone shares his or her feelings with you, he or she will trust you to share your ideas with him or her.

- Let it be known that you keep confidential information confidential!
- Practice understanding how people feel when they speak with you and reflect back this understanding.
- Share your honest feelings in a straightforward manner with those you can trust.

Hints on How to Limit Cathartic Communication

Managers and others often say that they listen to too much catharsis. They find it hard to turn off a conversation saturated with feelings when they have other important work to do. This is a good problem to have, but a problem nevertheless. The following suggestions may help.

- Express your appreciation to the person for sharing his or her feelings with you. If the person is very emotional, you may have to repeat it several times before you are heard.
- Reiterate or paraphrase the person's last statement using his or her tone of voice, rate of speech, volume, pitch, and gestures. Do this two or three times, if necessary, to make sure the person understood what you said.
- Tell the person that you would be glad to continue the conversation at a mutually agreed upon time and place. Let him or her know that you have to get back to a given task. By giving the person a specific time and place to look forward to, it is easier for him or her to disengage from the conversation.

SELF-ASSESSMENT EXERCISE Do you have enough cathartic communication with the important people in your personal and professional life? Do you need to limit cathartic communication with the people in your personal or professional life? In the space below, write the initials of the most important people in your personal and professional life.

Professional Life: _____ _____ _____

Personal Life: _____ _____ _____

Now put a plus sign by the initials of those with whom you want to increase your cathartic communication and put a minus sign by the initials of those with whom you need to limit cathartic communication. Think about when, where, and how you will do this.

INFORMATIONAL COMMUNICATION

The next two basic purposes of communication require the listener to be more critical. A major part of the communication you receive is informational. At this point you need to *be judgmental!*

Philosophers have suggested three criteria to help us judge the accuracy of information.

1. Is the information rationally coherent? Does the information fit into the rest of your life as you understand it? Rational coherence is an essential ingredient in evaluating information, but it is not an exclusive ingredient. You can start with the wrong assumption and still be rationally coherent.

A man suffering from a psychiatric problem thought that he was dead. Upon awaking each morning he told his wife that he was really dead. Unable to convince him that he was wrong, his wife sent him to a psychiatrist. The doctor asked him to read a text on the physical characteristics of a dead person.

The man returned to the psychiatrist for his second appointment more certain than ever that he was dead. The psychiatrist asked him, "According to the established text on the subject, do dead men bleed?"

"No," said the man, "I clearly recall reading that we do not."

"Give me your hand," ordered the psychiatrist. The man placed his hand in the psychiatrist's hand. The psychiatrist pricked the man's finger with a pin and blood appeared.

"What do you think of that?" asked the psychiatrist.

"What do you know," the man responded, "dead men do bleed!"

2. The second criterion in judging information is, "Is it factually valid?" This is the test of science. If this same event was replicated in the same fashion again and again would the results be the same?
3. The third criterion is logical consistency. If $1 + 1 = 2$ and $2 + 2 = 4$, then $1 + 1 + 1 + 1 = 4$. However, if the assumption is wrong in the beginning, the conclusion will be wrong. For example, to say that $2 + 2 = 5$, $3 + 3 = 7$, $4 + 4 = 9$, and $5 + 5 = 11$ is a perfectly logical statement, but it is wrong because it begins with a false assumption.

We need to hang on to whatever is valid and let go of everything that isn't. We need "roots" to ground us and "wings" to raise us to new vistas. Our criterion for judgment boils down to common sense. No one is assured of perfect understanding, accuracy, and response.

A new employee approached one of the women in the office with an important document in his hand. Pointing to the paper shredder, he asked her to show him how to operate it.

"Of course," she said. "You just turn the switch on, put your sheet of paper in here like this, and that's all there is to it."

As the machine devoured his document, the new employee thanked her for her help and then asked, "By the way, how many copies will this make?"[4]

LISTENING TO PERSUASION

As critical as you must be of the information received, you must be more critical of the attempts to persuade. Persuasive communication attempts to reinforce existing attitudes and beliefs, instill new attitudes and beliefs, or affect behaviors and actions. Listening to persuasion is such an important and broad issue for the listener that we will dedicate an entire chapter to it.

COMMUNICATIONS BONUS: THAT'S ENTERTAINMENT

A fifth purpose of communication is to entertain. This communication includes some of the arts and literature, as well as sports and all forms of humor. The multifaceted "light" side is one of life's necessities. Those of us who have become workaholics or have no time to read purely for pleasure, see a show, laugh at jokes, or exchange pleasantries with others, have shut ourselves off from many of the deepest joys and most profound experiences of life.

TRY IDENTIFYING THE FOUR BASIC PURPOSES OF COMMUNICATION

This exercise illustrates how the four basic purposes of communication can be found in a typical five-minute conversation. Remember that it is important to determine why another person is speaking to you in order to correctly interpret the meaning and decide how to respond.

Assess Your Recognition of Purpose of Communication

The following situation, transcribed from a conversation in one of our Fortune 500 companies, includes the four purposes of communication.[5] The conversation has been divided into paragraphs. Read through the conversation and follow the instructions.

Place a "P" after any paragraph that is primarily PHATIC communication.

Place a "C" after any paragraph that is primarily CATHARTIC communication.

Place an "I" after any paragraph that is primarily INFORMATIONAL communication.

And, place a "PS" after any paragraph that is primarily PERSUASIVE communication.

SETTING: An office, one person is sitting at a desk working; another enters.

I.   Tom (Seated): "Hi, Cathy. Good morning."

Cathy: "Good morning. How's everything?"

Tom: "Good."

Cathy: "How's your son? I understand he was in an accident."

Tom: "Fine. He was very lucky. We thought his arm was broken, but fortunately it wasn't."

Cathy: "Is he still in the hospital?"

Tom: "No, he was only in for a day. Right now he just has to be careful and not use the arm for a few days."

Cathy: "I'm glad to hear that."

What do you think is the overall purpose of this segment of the conversation: Phatic, Cathartic, Informational, or Persuasive? __

II.   Tom: "How are things in the department?"

        Cathy: "A mess. I had three out today. I can't believe these people. I'm killing myself out there and they don't even bother to show up."

        Tom: "I know. It can be murder trying to run your department with key people out."

        Cathy: "You know I took Larry into my office last week and talked to him for ten minutes about calling in when he's going to be late. Do you know that he's been out two days without calling in?"

        Tom: "Did you call his house?"

        Cathy: "What's the use? He always comes up with some stupid excuse. I tell you, sometimes I get so frustrated that I just feel like throwing in the towel. You treat 'em nice and they walk all over you. You're firm with them and they think you're a scrooge."

        Tom: "Hey Cathy, this is a tough business. I can understand your frustrations."

What do you think the basic purpose of this segment of the conversation is? ___

III.   Cathy: "Yeah, I'm sorry about dumping on you. Listen, the reason I came in was to ask about tuition reimbursement for a course I took."

        Tom (Pulling out some papers): "Just fill these out. Be sure to include the title of the course, the college where you'll take the course, and the date the course starts."

What do you think the basic purpose of this segment of the conversation is? ___

IV.   Cathy: "Thanks. I have a bit of a problem."

        Tom: "What's that?"

        Cathy: "Well you see, I took a management course already at a local college. Would it be all right for me to apply for credit now?"

Tom: "I'm afraid not. You must have prior approval to receive tuition credit."

Cathy: "What difference does it make?"

Tom: "Well, the course you took may not be the appropriate one for you to have taken."

Cathy: "But what if it was the right course to take? I checked with some other managers in my position, and they told me that they had this same course approved. I'm sure that this one is the right course for me to take."

Tom: "Well, I'm sorry, Cathy, but the procedure is to contact our office before you take the course."

Cathy: "But what difference does it make? It was the right course! I don't see why I should have to lose $400 because 'that's the procedure.' I can't believe this place. You try to improve yourself, and they just slap you in the face. Can't you bend the rules just this once?"

Tom: "Cathy, look. I can't bend the rules. We need prior approval because we are given only a certain budget, and we can't go over it. If we let you through, this sets a precedent, and we'll go out of business here."

What do you think the basic purpose of this segment of the conversation is? ___

V.   Cathy: "That's the most ridiculous thing I have ever heard. I've worked hard in this place. I never come in late. I do my job and this is what I get. Look at all those people abusing the system. You pat them on the back and ask them what you can do for them, but good employees like me get nothing. If this keeps up you won't have a single good employee in this place."

What do you think the basic purpose of the final segment of this conversation is? ___

As the above exercise illustrates, the purposes in conversations change. Consequently, our response to the speaker changes to correspond with the changing motive of the speaker.

Answers: I (P) Phatic, II (C) Cathartic, III (I) Informational, IV (PS) Persuasive, V (C) Cathartic.

Small talk is not bad. It forms the basis of understanding between people. Catharsis takes place when someone is "getting a load off his or her chest." The best reaction is often silence and sympathy, or empathy. Let the talker get it out, don't interrupt, and don't take it personally. Learn to recognize someone who is "all business" and only has time for informational conversation. Remain open-minded towards the person trying to persuade you. Don't make up your mind before the person finishes speaking.

F I V E

Identify and Repair Breakdowns in Listening

*The greatest problem in communication is the
illusion that it has been accomplished.*
—Daniel Davenport

ou can't fix a breakdown in communication until
you find the break.

On a passenger train traveling from Kansas City
to Houston, a rich oil man found a steward and paid
him $100 to make sure he got off in Dallas. An earth-
shaking deal depended on it. "No matter what I do
or say, just get me off!" Sometime later he left his
plush recliner to go to the rest room. When he
returned another businessman had taken his seat,
so he took another seat and fell asleep. Suddenly he
awoke and asked where he was. He discovered that
the train was pulling into Houston. He found the
steward and throttled him, banged him against the
wall, yelled, screamed, and raved. Finally, he hur-
ried off to catch a plane to Dallas. A second steward
came up and said, "I've never seen anybody so
mad!" The first steward answered, "That wasn't so
bad—you should have seen the guy I put off the
train in Dallas!"

Not every breakdown in communication results in a lost business deal, but it does cause some degree of loss in time, relationships, and effort. Communication breakdowns can be diagnosed and potentially corrected by studiously applying the S.I.E.R. formula.[1] This formula was presented by Dr. Lyman Steil and associates Drs. Kitty Watson and Larry Barker in the book *Effective Listening, Key to Your Success* and Dr. Steil's other listening books. It is an excellent diagnostic tool for interpreting past situations, an application tool for use in the present, and a planning tool for preparing for future communication. (See Figure 5.1.)

Figure 5.1.   Identify breakdowns in communication using the S.I.E.R. Formula.

Figure 5.2. Don't fight for air time—wait until the
speaker is finished.

Don't cut off communication by interrupting or responding in an inappropriate way; instead, hold your fire. Don't
come out swinging, looking for an argument, or trying to convince the other person. Instead of fighting for air space, allow
the person to say what he or she has to say, and communicate
your understanding of what has been said. Then you will have
an opportunity to say what you need to say. People will be
more receptive to your input when you have respectfully received theirs. Learn to apply Steil's simple S.I.E.R. formula.

The acronym S.I.E.R. for "Success in Everyday Relationships" makes Dr. Steil's formula easy to remember. However,
there are two elements that he perceives to be inherent in his
formula. The often overlooked skills of *Preparation* for listening and *Synchronization* with the speaker need to be named
and emphasized.[2] Less than half of the individuals whose listening skills we have analyzed deal adequately with these two
elements.

THE P.S.S.I.E.R. MODEL

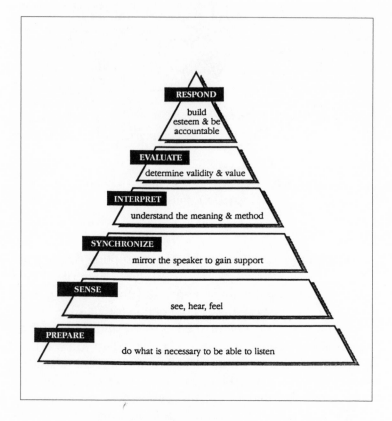

Figure 5.3. The P.S.S.I.E.R. Model—Successful communication breakdowns.

Prepare

The foundation for all success is 80 percent preparation and 20 percent application. Preparing means doing everything necessary so you can listen. Like any good investment, preparing to listen pays big dividends. The big payoff may not come immediately, but it will develop over a period of time. By developing the habit of preparing, you gradually build up your investment. President Abraham Lincoln said, "I spend one-third of my preparation in preparing for what I will say to the other person. I spend two-thirds of my preparation in anticipating what the other person will say to me."[3] Here is an example of a breakdown in listening on the preparation level.

George and Joanne are working together on a new process. They received a memo saying that a third person with experience on similar projects was joining their team. This person had several innovative ideas, and the memo explained three of the most significant ones. The following conversation took place a week after the memo was delivered.

> George: "Hi, Joanne, I saw your door open and thought I'd take the opportunity to discuss the new process with you."
>
> Joanne: "Come in, George. I have been anxious to get your reaction to several suggestions that Bill made."
>
> George (Surprised): "What suggestions, Joanne? I didn't know Bill had anything to do with this project."

George would have been informed if he had spent five minutes reading the memo and preparing. Instead, he stole time from Joanne since she had to explain Bill's ideas.

PREPARATION SELF-CHECK How often are you prepared to listen? Review the following statements and check the items that need attention.

— I try to get sufficient rest before important meetings.
— I learn as much as possible about an individual or subject before the meeting.

___ I make a mental note, or list unfamiliar subjects and words that I hear from individuals with whom I have frequent conversations.

___ I carefully choose a place in a conference or other listening situation that will minimize distractions and optimize my ability to listen.

___ I plan important conversations for the appropriate time and place.

___ I anticipate what emotionally laden subjects, people, or terms might come up in a conversation, and then practice controlling myself.

___ I hold all calls during important meetings.

___ I have a pen and paper in hand when I answer the telephone.

Sense

Hearing, seeing, feeling, and even smelling what a person says is sensing the communication. Many of the breakdowns in communication occur at the sense level. We didn't hear, see, or feel what the speaker communicated. We have to be highly selective on this level because we could never survive all the sensory input of human communication, let alone the meaningful noise of our environment. To protect ourselves from the glut of sound, we learn to discriminate and respond to selected frequencies and qualities of sound. We are also environmentally, relationally, and culturally selective; we automatically tune things out on each of these levels.

Sensing is also affected by interest, emotion, and bias. As a result, we build habits that can militate against our hearing many things that are or will be important to our lives. We cannot listen to everything, but we can try to be flexible and strengthen our ability to hear against the hardening of our mental arteries. Nationwide panic resulted on October 30, 1938, from Orson Welles's broadcast of the "War of the

Worlds." Listeners believed aliens from Mars had invaded New Jersey. Where did the communication breakdown occur? People failed to sense the repeated warnings of a fictitious broadcast. Their mind-set caused them to hear selectively.

A BREAKDOWN OF LISTENING AT THE SENSE LEVEL The general manager and supervisor had a lengthy morning meeting. At the conclusion of the meeting the general manager said, "By the way, that meeting has been changed to 2:30. It was 3:30. Did you get that?"

Supervisor: "Yeah, I got it."

(However, the supervisor arrived at the meeting at 3:30.)

General Manager: "Where were you? The meeting was at 2:30."

Supervisor: "You told me the meeting was at 3:30."

Clearly, the supervisor did not hear the words spoken by the general manager.

SENSING SELF-ASSESSMENT Do you sense everything necessary to get on the same wavelength with the speaker? Review the following statements and check the items that need attention.

___ During conversation, I look at the speaker as much as possible without staring.

___ I am aware of changes in a person's rate, pitch, and tone of speech.

___ I am aware of the feelings that the speaker is conveying or not conveying, e.g., anger, fear, sadness, happiness, surprise, disgust, or neutrality.

___ It is easy for me to pay attention to someone when I am sad, angry, or excited.

___ I am conscious of changes in a person's eye movements, facial expressions, posture, and gestures.

___ If I cannot avoid and/or remove environmental distractions, I concentrate more intently on the speaker.

Synchronize

Synchronizing is gaining rapport with the speaker by adopting a similar body stance, and vocal and facial cues. This skill is least understood by the hundreds of managers and professionals whose skills have been analyzed by our computerized listening inventory.

You cannot synchronize unless you have sensed what the person is conveying. Getting in "sync" is automatic if you sincerely concentrate on seeing, hearing, and feeling what the speaker is saying. Personality conflicts most often arise from differences in communication style resulting in a lack of synchronization. We are automatically in "sync" with those who are like us. We tend to appreciate and feel comfortable with those who communicate like us, and we are uncomfortable and discontent with those who do not. Without a conscious effort, we often break the communication link at this level with those who communicate differently from us.

COMMUNICATION BREAKDOWN AT THE SYNCHRONIZING LEVEL
Dave and Lydia have worked together in development for six months. The following conversation transpired at the conclusion of a meeting about their joint project. The "report" mentioned was submitted by the marketing department as a summary of the application of their work.

Dave: "I didn't like the organization of the report."
Lydia: "Come on, Dave, you don't mean *that* bothered you?"
Dave: "So long, Lydia, I have to be going."
Lydia: "Now you have to leave? What's the hurry?"
Dave: "Bye, Lydia."

Communication without rapport is difficult and uncomfortable. If Lydia had sincerely reflected Dave's feelings in an understanding manner before disagreeing with him, she would have established rapport and the conversation could have been constructive. Instead, Dave went away angry and Lydia was confused.

SYNCHRONIZE SELF-ASSESSMENT How often do you suffer a breakdown in communication at the synchronization level? These breakdowns are often called "personality conflicts." They are a mismatch in communication style. Review the following items and ask yourself how often you have tried these techniques with a personality "mismatch."

   I share experiences when I feel the same emotion that the
      speaker is feeling.
   I communicate an understanding of the thoughts and feel-
      ings of others, before stating a contrary position.
   I do not try to change the subject until either the speaker
      is finished or I have the speaker's permission to change
      the subject.
   When I am aware that we don't have rapport, I attempt to
      match my gestures to the style and intensity of the
      speaker.
   While communicating with different personality types, I
      match my facial expression to that of the speaker.
   When seeking rapport, I match my rate of speech, tone of
      voice, pitch, and modulation to that of the speaker.

Interpret

If the message is not sensed and synchronized, it cannot be accurately interpreted. To interpret is to understand the meaning of what the speaker is saying. To interpret accurately does not mean that we agree with the speaker. The problem most people have is that they interpret what is being said without adequate preparation. They haven't sensed what is being said nor have they synchronized with the speaker. Without proper preparation, our prejudices, backgrounds, presuppositions, and experiences produce a reflex causing us to anticipate what we think is going to be said. Untrained listeners are usually less than half right about what they anticipate is going to be said.

The fact that we understand as much as we do is phenomenal. We do not comprehend how understanding happens. This ability is deeply buried in the matrix of the human brain, the terra incognita of the universe. How any child learns to speak and understand, simply by listening to the voices of his language community, is a miracle that no amount of study and thought has explained. How anyone, child or adult, can understand any language in all its complexity and amazing variety is equally inexplicable and even more mysterious. Just to utter all the possible English sentences of twenty words would require ten trillion years. We utter sentences from time to time that have never been heard on earth. In addition, we live to some degree in a world of our own; few events or objects mean exactly the same thing to everyone.

To see the distinction between interpreting and sensing or synchronizing, carefully think about this statement. "A caterpillar is eating everything in sight!" Answer the following questions about your understanding of the caterpillar and what it is doing. Remember words comprise only 7 percent of the message.

1. When you think of the caterpillar, is it a big one or a small one? How much would you estimate that it weighs?
2. How much noise is it making while it is "eating"?
3. Describe the sound.

Thousands of people in our workshops have pictured a caterpillar weighing an ounce or so, chewing leaves, and making little or no sound at all. But the caterpillar I had in mind weighs thousands of pounds and is made by a manufacturer of heavy equipment. Its engine is roaring while it digs a large hole. We all see or hear the same message, but we interpret it differently. I believe that most breakdowns in communication take place before or at this level in the model.

When you identify where a breakdown in communication takes place, you can work on solving the problem. When looking at the P.S.S.I.E.R. model, always go to the base of the triangle and work your way from the bottom up. The first question to ask is, "Was the listener prepared to listen?" If you can answer yes to this question, move on to the next level. "Did the listener see, hear, and feel what the speaker said?" Answering yes to this question enables you to go on. "Did the listener get in sync with the speaker?" If the answer is no at this level or any of the lower levels, a domino effect follows with breakdowns coming at the higher levels. At the interpretation level ask the listener if he or she understood what was seen, heard, and felt? By asking these questions you will learn to recognize the difference between being prepared to listen, sensing a message, synchronizing with the messenger, and understanding what the message means. Each step in the model is a prerequisite to the next. You also need to learn how to interpret the purpose behind the message.

COMMUNICATION BREAKDOWNS AT THE INTERPRETATION LEVEL The following conversation took place in a major automaker's plant. It occurred at the end of a discussion about miscellaneous things that could have been done easily by the next day.[4]

> Maria: "Listen, Harry, how about having your people finish these cost studies for me?"
> Harry: "I can handle that."
> (Next day)
> Maria: "Harry, did you finish those cost studies?"

Harry: "No."

Maria: "Why not? You said you would."

Harry: "I did not."

Maria: "What are you talking about? You told me yesterday that you would finish them."

Harry: "What are you talking about? I never said anything of the kind."

Maria heard what Harry said, but she thought, "I can handle that" meant that Harry would do it by the next day. Harry meant that he was capable of doing it, but not that he would do it. Both parties were sincere. Both were sincerely wrong about what the other intended to convey.

The next breakdown is a misunderstanding between two co-workers. The third party, Bob, the manager, is trying to heal a fractured relationship between Jim and Vicky.[5]

Bob (On phone): "Listen, Jim. I think the best way to clear up this problem is for you and Vicky to get together."

Jim: "I agree."

Bob: "OK, then. I'll talk to you later to find out how it turned out."

(Two days later)

Bob (As a woman walks into his office): "Hello, Vicky."

Vicky: "Hi! Hey, you know, Jim never called me."

Bob: "Really! (Picking up the phone) I'll call him. (Dialing) Hello, Jim. This is Bob. I have Vicky here in my office, and she tells me you haven't called her yet."

Jim: "I wasn't supposed to call her. She was supposed to call me. She started this whole thing. Why would I call her to set up a meeting?"

In this breakdown Jim heard the actual words used by Bob, but he interpreted them differently than Vicky did.

INTERPRETATION SELF-ASSESSMENT Do you accurately understand what the speaker means by what he or she is intending to convey? Review the following statements and check the items that need attention.

— I ask speakers to clarify what I do not understand.

— I restate or paraphrase what a speaker has said to make certain that I have understood the individual.

— I can tell when someone is trying to persuade me.

— I ask questions to encourage individuals to express their opinions.

— I listen for a speaker's major ideas and do not get lost in the details.

— I pay more attention to a speaker's content than to his or her appearance and manner of delivery.

Evaluate

> *. . . nobody can judge a case unless he listens*
> *to all the arguments on both sides.*
> —*St. Thomas Aquinas*

If you conclude that the message was sensed, the messenger and you are in "sync," and the message was understood, proceed to the evaluation level. Evaluation is the watchdog, the sentinel standing at the gate that "puts a value" on what we hear, have heard, and understood. Evaluation is affected by unconscious assumptions. For example, you may reject a communication because of the way the speaker is dressed.

Evaluation is also affected by beliefs and expectations. We tend to respond to others with our evaluation before we have understood the message. Carl Rogers, Eli Porter, Sr., and associates tested professionals to find out what kind of response was given first: evaluation, interpretation, support, probing, or understanding. "They are most commonly given, they discovered, in that order. Evaluation. . . came first."[6] How you evaluate someone determines how well you are able to listen to that person and how much you can draw out of him or her. You are aware of a "self-fulfilled prophecy." People usually produce what we expect of them. Frequently you think you heard what you expected to hear! In evaluation, you determine the validity and the immediate or long-term value of what is communicated. Our evaluation can be positive or negative; it can involve giving a message too much importance or not enough.

Effective listeners sometimes disagree with the speaker. The danger lies in disagreeing before you fully understand. To understand does not mean that you agree, so when you disagree, try to disagree agreeably.

Figure 5.4.   Effective listeners make appropriate
evaluations.

Follow these basic principles at the evaluation level. First, is the information valuable to you? Is it relevant? This may be difficult to determine because you don't know what the future holds. It may be necessary to delay a final determination of its value for a more deliberate analysis, particularly when the information is very long, complicated, or critical.

Secondly, is the information valid? Is it accurate? Remember that philosophers use three basic principles to determine the validity of information. (See Chapter 4: Informational Communication.) Following the three principles can help us.

1. Determine if the "facts" are demonstrable in your experience or in the experience of an expert you can trust.
2. Determine if the content of the message can be supported by consistent logic. Even though the presentation is logical, it is still possible to end up with a wrong conclusion if the speaker begins with a wrong assumption.
3. Determine if the "facts" are relevant to the discussion.

For example, "Miss America," who was born with a flawless complexion, may advertise the value of a particular skin cream for her skin care. Since genetics, not the cream, are responsible for her perfect condition, Miss America's perfect skin is irrelevant to the product. Similarly, you might question whether athletes know more about soft drinks or beer than the man or woman next door. Effective listeners are aware of the relevance or irrelevance of the "facts" in a conversation. Usually two of the three criteria listed above must be met in order to feel the message has validity.

Generally, we are hooked into listening because we accept the validity of the message. Psycholinguist Suzette Haden Elgin subscribes to cognitive scientist George Miller's "Law." Miller's "Law" is "In order to understand what another person is saying, you must assume it is true and try to imagine what it could be true of."[7] But once you determine that the message is probably valid, you must decide if it has any value to you. This question is sometimes more difficult to answer than the validity question. An extended period of time may pass before you can profitably use the information. To determine the value of the message, it may be necessary to delay a final evaluation for a more deliberate analysis, particularly when the information is very long, complicated, or critical.

COMMUNICATION BREAKDOWNS AT THE EVALUATION LEVEL

> George: "Bill, please finish up the accounting procedure report."
>
> Bill: "OK, George."

At the end of the day George asks, "Will you bring the accounting procedure report to my office, Bill?" The report was not completed because Bill didn't give the information enough importance. He was tired and had been struggling with a problem employee and gave the order a low priority. What was the result of his improper evaluation? He was chewed out.

> Barbara: "Wayne, please get me the final figures as soon as possible."
>
> Wayne: "You bet, Barbara, I'll get them to you before lunch."

But Wayne spent too much time on the report and ignored his day-to-day responsibilities. He gave Barbara's request too much importance because that's what he thought she wanted him to do.

> Lin: "Terry, I need next Tuesday off for some personal business."
>
> Terry: "You can't have Tuesday off, that's a busy day for us."

Angered by the assistant manager's overbearing and insensitive attitude, Lin purposely works more slowly. Lin responded to her supervisor by giving his response a negative evaluation. This happens more frequently in the work-place than is imagined. Only 23 percent of our jobholders say that they are working up to their potential! It is generally believed that anger is caused by fear, which in turn is caused by loss. Grieving for a lost loved one is a form of anger. Similarly, whether we lose time, a friend, money, prestige, or an opportunity to take care of some "personal business," the result is the same; we become fearful and then angry.

EVALUATION SELF-ASSESSMENT Do you properly evaluate the information being sent? Review the following statements and check the items that need attention.

___ I weigh factual evidence carefully before I make a decision.

___ It is easy for me to pay attention to someone I don't like, as long as the person knows what he or she is talking about.

___ It is easy for me to disagree with someone I like very much.

___ Even though someone uses words that I find personally offensive, I am attentive to what he or she is saying.

___ When I am receiving criticism, I discern and admit to any element that is true.

___ I listen for a speaker's major ideas and do not get lost in the details.

___ I pay more attention to a speaker's content than to his or her appearance and manner of delivery.

___ I find something of value in what every speaker has to say.

___ I differentiate facts from opinions.

Respond

*The technique which I was obliged to develop in
those unimportant early posts has served me
in later years for my imperial audiences: to give
oneself totally to each person throughout the brief
duration of a hearing; to reduce the world for a
moment to this banker, that veteran, or that
widow; to accord to these individuals, each so
different though each confined naturally within
the narrow limits of a type, all the polite attention
which at the best moments one gives to oneself.*
—Roman Emperor Hadrian

Response is the apex of the P.S.S.I.E.R. model, and it is the ultimate measure of how well we listen. An effective listener answers a speaker's communication by communicating understanding of what was said and felt, and accepting responsibility for that understanding. In your response you feed back to the speaker your understanding of the other person's problems and needs, and take the responsibility to follow through. If a breakdown occurs at the response level, ask yourself, "Did the listener do what he or she decided to do? Did he or she forget to do it? Did he or she not have enough time, information, or ability to do it? Has the person done a poor job because of a lack of time, information, or ability?"

If you have the skill to fulfill all of the other prerequisites well but do not respond appropriately, you create a breakdown in communication. Reaction and response are not the same. A reaction is spontaneous and immediate; it omits preparation, the total sensing process, proper synchronization, accurate interpretation, and fair evaluation. A response, on the other hand, is thoughtful; it is based on proper preparation, sensing, synchronizing, interpretation, and evaluation.

The ultimate listening goal is to make appropriate evaluations and responses. Avoid inappropriate responses and non-responses that can destroy relationships and communication. Response completes the cycle of communication by indicating, in an appropriate way, that you have understood.

Try to identify where the breakdown in communication occurs in the following stories.

A bar owner locked up his place at 2:00 a.m. and went home to sleep. He had been in bed only a few minutes when the phone rang. "What time do you open in the morning?" he heard an obviously inebriated man inquire.

The owner was so furious, he slammed down the receiver and went back to bed. A few minutes later there was another call and he heard the same voice ask the same question. "Listen," the owner shouted, "there's no sense in asking me what time I open because I wouldn't let a person in your condition in—"

"I don't want to get in," the caller interjected. "I want to get out."[8]

A disheartened Edsel dealer was about to commit suicide. Walking down an alley he spied a bottle and decided to take a last drink. When he opened the bottle a genie appeared and offered one wish. "I want to be a foreign car dealer in a major city," pled the dealer.

Poof!—He's an Edsel dealer in Tokyo.

Where is the breakdown in communication?

As a responder it is easy to get on someone's case and assume that they evaluated the communication differently than you and are going against your will. But they may never have understood what you said, or they may not have heard, felt, and seen what you said in the first place.

The words "response" and "responsibility" are close in meaning. We have a tendency to respond to others with evaluation before we have fulfilled the responsibility to understand the message. Remember that even professional listeners tend to evaluate the person before understanding the message.

An evaluation pushes the other person away. Whether it is approving or disapproving, evaluation is judgmental. Close-up videotapes of people conversing show that the face gives an unconscious shock signal when an evaluation is received. A vertical wrinkle appears between the eyes, for a split second, as the eyebrows pull together in the universal sign of anxiety or pain. No matter how subtle the judgment, it makes an impact, and the impact is the same whether you judge the person or his or her message.[9] Since evaluations given at the wrong time can prevent effective listening, it is important to learn the art of giving nonverbal responses that communicate understanding. Wait patiently for the appropriate time to vocalize your evaluative responses. Frequently, when the right time comes, the evaluation that seemed important earlier is no longer needed.

Similar strengths and weakness were found in individuals who were expected to rise higher in their organization but did not, and those who made it to the top. The difference most often cited between the two groups is that the derailed group is more insensitive to others. This is not the only reason for derailment. Some commit the "unforgivable sin," betraying a trust. "Betrayal" rarely has anything to do with honesty, which is a given. Rather, it is one-upping others or failure to follow through on promises. This wreaks havoc in terms of trust. Your responses tell who you are and what you think of others. They help people determine how much trust and confidence they can place in you.

RESPONSE SELF-ASSESSMENT Review the following statements and check the items that need attention.

__ I do not try to change the subject until either the speaker is finished or I have the speaker's permission to change the subject.

__ When I am receiving criticism, I discern and admit to any element that is true.

__ I do not interrupt until the speaker is finished. Then I pause, think, and respond.

__ I find something of value in what every speaker has to say.

__ In a conversation, I listen more than I speak.

__ I keep privately shared information confidential.

__ I try to raise the self-esteem of everyone I listen to.

__ I consistently follow through on what is expected of me after a conversation.

P.S.S.I.E.R. SAWTOOTH MODEL

This model expands the static, "frozen frame moment" to show how our interactions progress through time. As we switch back and forth between sender and receiver roles, we prepare, sense, synchronize, interpret, evaluate, and respond simultaneously. Communication becomes even more complex when you add other people to the conversation. (See Figure 5.5.)

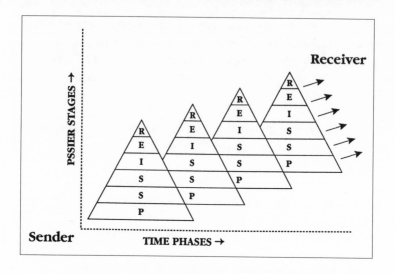

Figure 5.5. P.S.S.I.E.R. Sawtooth Process Model.

Learn to listen to the complete message, so you won't miss important information later. Otherwise, you will assume you already know what a person is going to say and fail to listen.

Communication problems are easier to solve if we can specifically identify where and how they occur. The P.S.S.I.E.R. model will help you do this. Prepare, Sense, Synchronize, Interpret, Evaluate, and then Respond.

S I X

Use the "RELATIONS" Model for Effective Listening

A word fitly spoken is like apples of gold in settings of silver.—King David

It is through experiencing your acceptance, respect, and appreciation that the other will become more open and honest with you, and thereby increase your ability to be helpful and to resolve possible problems and conflicts with the other.[1]
—Dr. Bernard Guerney

The "RELATIONS" model is a sure fire model to follow in developing effective listening skills and building positive relations. First we will discuss the model, and then we'll review the roadblocks that often hinder its use.

Jerry had an urgent need when she walked into her supervisor's office. "George, do you have a minute?" George barely looked up from his desk. "Oh, it's you again! Get to the point, Jerry, I'm in a hurry."

Jerry quit her job that day. Trying to communicate with George had become too stressful and unproductive. After fifteen years of service Jerry still liked her work, but her supervisor's abrasive manner was too much to handle. Her many attempts to build a relationship with her supervisor always led to a dead end. In spite of the difficult relationship, she always did her best job and tolerated this aggravation for two years.

Now she was getting an ulcer. Trying to work with her super was more difficult than it was worth.

Jerry is not alone in her reaction to job-related stress. Thousands of workers quit their jobs everyday because of similar circumstances. Broken relationships are a primary cause of stress and the main reason why employees leave their companies. Seventy-five percent of workers in the United States admit that they do not work up to their capacity.[2] Building better relationships through effective listening will increase worker satisfaction and productivity.

INITIALLY WITHHOLD JUDGMENT

Initially, when listening to a problem, try to show understanding and unquestioning acceptance of the other's views. "Even when you totally disagree with another's opinion or perception; even when you think the other person's feelings are based on false assumptions or will lead to regrettable actions, it is still possible to show the other respect, appreciation, and understanding. . . . In effect you are saying to the other person, whether I agree or disagree with you, I appreciate your willingness to share your thoughts with me. I will respect and value you as a person regardless of what feelings or motives or wishes you express, and regardless of whether or not I agree with your values or the realism of what you are telling me. I welcome your views because they give me a chance to understand you and, therefore, to relate better to you."[3] Before stating your opinion, it is best to first walk around in the other person's shoes.

The president of a company was constantly solving problems for his management team. He had no time for strategic planning. Even his weekends were filled with work. Every Monday his managers appeared in his office to ask for advice. Throughout the week he dispensed his wisdom, but invariably there were more problems than days in the week to solve them. When Saturday came he had several problems riding on his back like monkeys. Usually by Sunday he had the monkeys off his back, so he could begin fresh on Monday morning.

One Saturday, on an emergency run to the grocery store, he drove past the golf course and spotted his top managers enjoying each other's company on the eighteenth green. He asked himself how they could afford to spend the weekend playing golf and enjoying themselves when he, the boss, didn't have the time.

It's always a good idea to talk to yourself. One advantage of talking to yourself is that you know someone's listening! It's even a better idea to argue with yourself. You're only in trouble when you argue and lose! This corporate executive argued with himself and won. He realized that he was doing his managers' jobs. From now on, he would give them the responsibility and allow them the privilege of solving their own problems. After all, he had hired qualified people.

On Monday morning when the first manager entered his office with a problem, the president resisted the temptation to solve it. Instead he asked appropriate questions and insisted his subordinates report their conclusions to him. Each professional was held accountable for identifying and solving his or her own problems. The president discovered that this is the way to deal with highly-motivated, skilled professionals.

At the end of the week the president went home with his job done, and his managers felt that they had completed their work satisfactorily. His newfound skill of helping responsible professionals feed and care for the "monkeys" on their own backs revitalized his organization. This experience became the foundation of a popular workshop on how to help responsible managers take care of their own "monkeys."

Charlie Hugel, a retired executive vice-president from AT & T, exemplified this managerial skill. Charlie was responsible for hundreds of millions of dollars in revenue. More than 90 percent of his time was spent listening to subordinates analyze their problems. He asked the appropriate questions and reflected back his understanding of their thoughts and feelings. His managers solved their own problems. Way to go, Charlie!

Life is solving problems. Problems are normal. Most of us agree that we are better at solving our own problems than other people are. But we also know that sometimes it is helpful to discuss our problems with a good listener. Eighty percent of our problems will be easier to solve with the help of an attentive listener.

THE "RELATIONS" MODEL

Most people go through life without a good model of how to be an effective listener. The "RELATIONS" model for effective listening will provide you with a basic, effective map to get around the communication roadblocks. The "RELATIONS" acronym was coined by my associate, Dr. Ken Boa, and me. It includes the basic elements of an effective listening model and encapsulates the essence of what communication is about. Effective listening builds trusting relationships, and from trusting relationships comes greater productivity.

Practice the "RELATIONS" model with the five people you decided to build better relationships with and who were offended by your responses to their problems.

"R" Is for Relaxed Tension

A nonjudgmental, positive attitude helps the listener develop an awareness of communication purposes. When you are tense, it is more difficult to concentrate on what the speaker is saying. Tension causes you to think more about yourself and your response than about the speaker.

"E" Is for Eye Contact without Staring

A person's eye movements and the way the eyes dilate or don't dilate are an unconscious, nonverbal communication to you about what the person is thinking and feeling. If the person's eyes dilate, and the lighting in the room didn't change, it's because the person's emotions have probably been triggered. The emotion can be anger, fear, or joy. You may not be certain which emotion was touched, but you can be certain that an emotion was affected.

Look directly at the speaker and appear to be attentive. If you have trouble looking at the speaker's eyes, look at his or her forehead. From several feet away, the speaker usually cannot tell the difference. By observing the speaker's eyes you will be looking at the "light of his or her soul." The eyes can tell you much about what the speaker really means when he or she is talking. Eye contact is important, but it is true that in some cultures eye contact is rude.

"L" Is for Lean in Toward the Speaker

This body stance communicates an openness to the speaker and encourages him or her to say more. Proxemics, the study of space and human relations to space, is very revealing. In some cultures people like to be very close to each other when they talk. In Greece, Brazil, and Japan, proximity of less than three feet from the speaker is normal among members of the same sex. Backing away from the speaker is considered an insult. In Germany and some Scandinavian countries, three feet would be too close in many business situations. Sensitivity to distance requires individual adjustment to find the optimum distance that is most comfortable for the other person.

"A" Is for Active Silence

Without saying anything verbally, this skill communicates to the speaker that you are listening, thinking, and trying to

Figure 6.1. Effective listeners lean toward the speaker.

understand what he or she is saying. Usually a silence of two or three seconds is sufficient to determine if the speaker is finished and wants you to respond verbally. After this flicker of silence in the conversation, the good stuff comes out. The speaker ends a thought, sees that you're really listening, and proceeds with what he or she *really* wanted to say. Remain attentive and think about what the speaker is saying. Put on your "EARS"; silently Evaluate, Anticipate, Review, and Summarize. Do not interrupt. Wait until the speaker is finished and then think, pause, and respond.

"T" Is for Tell Me More
Use nonverbal feedback to encourage the speaker to continue. When you match the intensity and manner of the speaker with facial expressions, gestures, nods, and responses like "uh-huh, oh, and mm-hmm," you encourage him or her to continue.

"I" Is for Involved Feedback
Use verbal responses to involve yourself with the thought process and feelings of the speaker. Reiterate some of the same

words he or she uses and paraphrase some of the thoughts. Ask appropriate questions for clarification. Ask yourself, "How would I feel if I were the speaker?" Then take a chance and tell the speaker how you think he or she feels. Stand ready to be corrected if you are inaccurate.

"O" Is for Open Posture

Your arms may be crossed tightly across your chest because you're cold or tired. But, subliminally, this stance can create the impression that you're closed to what the person is saying. Body language is a very important means of communication and it can signal 4,000 intelligible messages during a typical day. As the nonverbal communications are sent out, a person subliminally responds. Uncross your arms to demonstrate that you are receptive. Subconsciously this helps the speaker believe that you are open to his or her thoughts and feelings, and it enables the speaker to be more open with you.

"N" Is for Noise Control

Do not let internal and external noises distort the message or prevent you from listening to the speaker's message. Some internal "noises" are caused by physiological problems such as a headache or fatigue. Psychological "noises" are created by a recent argument or by emotionally charged words or subject matter, whether positive or negative. External "noises" include other people talking, a telephone ringing, a television left on, or an air conditioner turning on and off. Try to recognize the noise and then either eliminate it or ignore it.

"S" Is for Squared Off

"Square off" or directly face the speaker. This position not only demonstrates interest, but it enables you to see and hear the speaker much better. Obviously there are occasions when it is not possible to "square off," for example, when you are walking side by side. If you and another person sit across from each other at a desk, you are squared off, but the desk is a barrier. If possible, set a chair alongside your desk, so you don't have the barrier separating you and the other person.

HOW TO OVERCOME THE "DIRTY DOZEN ROADBLOCKS TO EFFECTIVE LISTENING"

Dr. Rich Walters identified the "Dirty Dozen Roadblocks to Effective Listening."[4] These are usually hindrances we must overcome to allow others to solve their own problems. Just as informative road signs that are set up in the right place and at the right time can be helpful on a journey, the "dirty dozen roadblocks" can also be helpful. Most of us overuse and misuse responses. It is imperative to build better communication, develop positive relationships, and increase productivity. Examine the list below, identify the responses overused, and remove the roadblocks.

A good listener helps people solve their own problems. He resists setting up conversational roadblocks. Instead, he makes his responses "road signs" that help the speaker see and hear his own thoughts and feelings.

You will accomplish more and build better relationships by allowing others to arrive at their own conclusions. The "dirty dozen roadblocks" can be "stepping stones" to effective communication, positive relationships, and greater productivity. Like fine spices, when used properly, they can benefit a conversation. Seventy-five percent of the time people are better off solving their own problems, and 99 percent of the time they will be more responsive to our suggestions when we demonstrate an understanding of what they think and feel.

"Before responding, ask yourself five questions to put yourself in the speaker's place. If I were the speaker:

1. Would I be thinking positively or negatively about myself?
2. What would I be feeling?
3. What would I be wishing?
4. What would I be thinking about doing?
5. What conflicts would I be experiencing?"[5]

Two yellow lights flash at this juncture. If you consistently respond empathetically, you may become the other's counselor. To avoid this type of relationship, use more "seasoning" in your responses. If you respond mechanically instead of naturally, you will undo the trust you are trying to build.

Find the Roadblocks to Your Communication Success

Examine the twelve "roadblocks" listed below, and then follow these three steps.

1. Check the roadblock responses that most often characterize you.
2. Think about the five people with whom you plan to improve your communication relationship. Write the initials of the person(s) you offend with these responses.
3. Imagine the situation and write a response that you prefer to use from now on. A suggested response is given as an example.

Notice that roadblocks one through five are situations where you refuse to recognize that the person is capable of handling his or her own problems.

Roadblock #1: Giving direction and commanding. The drill sergeant in you tells the other person to do something, gives orders, or commands, instead of reflecting back an understanding of his or her problem.

Statement: "Adding a new shift to the floor is going to double our administrative responsibilities."

Roadblock: "Be grateful for the increased productivity and stop complaining."

Initials: _____

A Suggested Response: "You are glad that the company is doing well, but you are concerned that you are getting more than your share of the added work."

Your Response: _____

Roadblock #2: Advising, suggesting, offering solutions, and telling the other person how to solve his or her problems. In this roadblock, you play the role of the parent and communicate condescension to the speaker.

Statement: "My boss doesn't approve of his people leaving even two minutes early."

Roadblock: "If for any reason you must leave early, check with your boss early in the day and request permission. Make sure you agree to come in early or to stay late the following day to make up the time."

Initials: _____

A Suggested Response: "You are concerned about your boss's attitude toward those who leave early."

Your Response: _____

Roadblock #3: Warning, admonishing, and threatening. These roadblocks tell the other person that negative consequences will occur if he does something. You allude to the use of your power.

Statement: "What is the meaning of that memo we received in the mail this morning? I have a right to know and I'm going to start asking questions."

Roadblock: "Curiosity killed the cat. You start asking a lot of questions and you'll get yourself in trouble."

Initials: _____

A Suggested Response: "You feel the memo was too vague and raised some issues you have a right to know about."

Your Response: _____

Roadblock #4: Moralizing and preaching. In this roadblock you assume the superior role of a prophet with divine insight.

Statement: "Cutting out our overtime without warning is a bummer."

Roadblock: "You should be glad you have a job!"

Initials: _____

A Suggested Response: "You feel they should have prepared you for the added responsibility."

Your Response: _____

Roadblock #5: Persuading, arguing, and lecturing. You use "facts," counter arguments, logic, and information to influence the speaker with your own opinions instead of empathizing with the speaker.

Statement: "I have two candidates for the new secretarial position. I'm going to choose youth over experience. You can't teach an old dog new tricks."

Roadblock: "If you had more information you wouldn't make that mistake. First, the younger candidate has not yet shown the ability to fit into the culture. You don't even know if she is capable of doing the work. Second, the older candidate has proven her ability and adaptability. She has changed and grown with each new assignment over the past ten years."

Initials: _____

A Suggested Response: "Of the two candidates, you believe the youngest has the best chance of adapting to the new position."

Your Response: _____

Roadblocks six through ten are personal "put-downs" and real ego crushers. In these responses, the speaker is given less respect than in the first five responses. He or she is misunderstood and the relationship is worse than if he or she hadn't tried to share the problem.

Roadblock #6: Judging, criticizing, disagreeing, and blaming. In this response the speaker is rejected. Negative judgments were made of the person's character, not of his or her analysis of the problem being shared.

Statement: "My performance appraisal was a shock."

Roadblock: "A real professional knows what his or her manager thinks of his or her work. You just haven't been paying attention."

Initials: _____

A Suggested Response: "You were taken by surprise."

Your Response: _____

Roadblock #7: Inappropriate praise. In this response, you flatter the speaker or offer a positive evaluation or judgment without listening, thereby short-circuiting the communication.

You imply that what the speaker is saying is so embarrassing that he or she shouldn't be heard.

Statement: "My spouse and I are having a tough time. We don't have much to say to each other anymore."

Roadblock: "I heard about the report you turned in last week. Great job."

Initials: _____

A Suggested Response: "It sounds like things are tough at home."

Your Response: _____

Roadblock #8: Name-calling, ridiculing, and shaming. This response makes the speaker feel foolish, and often stereotypes or categorizes him or her. This is the mugger in action, catching our prey unaware.

Statement: "Look at the awful way that guy dresses. You'd think he would know better."

Roadblock: "You guys that criticize are all alike. Look at yourselves sometime. You're all guilty of the problem you see in others."

Initials: _____

A Suggested Response: "You'd like to see a guy in his position dress more appropriately."

Your Response: _____

Responses nine through twelve implicitly deny that a problem even exists. We assume "it's just the person's imagination."

Roadblock #9: Focusing on the person and not the problem. In this response you play the part of a "psychiatrist," telling a person what his motives are, or analyzing why he or she is doing or saying something.

Statement: "When is this fatigue going to stop! I have been tired ever since the vacation."

Roadblock: "I think you're really saying that you don't like your work."

Initials: _____

A Suggested Response: "You must really miss your old energy level. It's tough not knowing when you will feel like yourself again."

Your Response: _____

Roadblock #10: Withdrawing, distracting, and humoring. This response attempts to distract the individual from the problem, instead of helping him or her explain it. Misused "humor" is like vinegar on an open wound.

Statement: "It cost more to repair my car than it's worth."

Roadblock: "Funny, isn't it, that beauty's only skin deep, but ugly's to the bone. Beauty fades away, but ugly holds its own. Ha, Ha!"

Initials: _____

A Suggested Response: "You feel like you've been taken for a ride on that repair bill."

Your Response: _____

Roadblock #11: Probing, questioning, interrogating, putting the person on the defensive, or incorrectly assuming the problem. In this response you act like the detective or prosecuting attorney trying to find motives or causes, and searching for more information to help solve the problem.

Statement: "My assistant was late three times last week."

Roadblock: "Did you ask him to set his alarm a few minutes earlier?"

Initials: _____

A Suggested Response: "Three times in one week, that's frustrating."
Your Response: _____

Roadblock #12: Patronizing and condescending. You try to make the other person feel better, talk him out of his feelings, make his feelings go away, deny the strength of his feelings, and perform like a magician.
Statement: "I'm so angry I could chew nails. Everyone gets recognition for their work except me."
Roadblock: "It's too bad that a person like you gets treated this way. But cheer up, we all go through this sometime."
Initials: _____
A Suggested Response: "You recognize the value of your work; it makes you angry that others don't see it also."
Your Response: _____

Now you've identified some roadblocks and you know with whom to use them. You've thought through some responses and have made progress. Listen for the opportunity to respond in this way and notice how it opens communication.

You can build better relationships by using the "RELATIONS" model, or you can continue to set up roadblocks. The skills outlined above work. Practice the "RELATIONS" model with a friend and then move on to riskier relationships. Enjoy the benefits of principles proven true by thousands of successful associates.

S E V E N

Learn to Control Your Emotions When Listening

A man who can control his emotions is stronger than a warrior who can capture a city.
—*King Solomon*

He who reigns within himself, rules passions, desires and fears, and is more than a king.
—*John Milton*

Each of us is an impregnable fortress that can be laid waste only from within.—*Timothy J. Flynn*

Emotion brings color, meaning, fulfillment, and purpose to our lives. Through our emotions we taste the worst or the best of life. Emotions pull us down and lift us up. Emotional expression can turn monotonous, humdrum tasks into beautiful and rich experiences. Without emotion, life would be devoid of pain and zest.

Hundreds of millions of dollars are spent each year finding out what touches your emotions. Merchandisers use this information to push your emotional button, hoping to induce a particular action. The world of market research is rife with organizations and individuals who are well-trained, highly skilled, and motivated to discover the emotional triggers of others.

Sometimes people unconsciously touch your emotions. Think about your home life; who touches your emotions at home? Does this person know that he or she touches your emotions? Is he or she conscious of the words or actions that touch you? How do you respond when your emotions are affected? Think about your professional life. Most business teams are made up of different personalities with different ways of expressing feelings. Do the differences help or hinder you on the job?

Everyone has emotional triggers. When emotions go up, rationality goes down. "Anyone who is in a position to know more about your emotional triggers than you do is in a position to control you."[1] Controlling your emotions will free you to be all that you can possibly be.

EMOTIONS CAN BRING GAIN OR PAIN

The legendary football coach Vince Lombardi shared with corporation leader Lee Iacocca how important emotions are to the success of a team. When talent, discipline, and coaching are about equal, emotion makes the difference. "If you are going to play together as a team, you've got to care for one another. You've got to *love* each other. The difference between mediocrity and greatness is the feeling these guys have for each other. . . . It's the same thing whether you are running a ball club or a corporation."[2]

He was working under the car when the bumper slid off the jack and pinned him under 1,500 pounds. He would have been doomed had his 112-pound mother not reached down and lifted the car off him. (Ripley's *Believe it or Not*)

Every business and every person faces 1,500-pound problems with 112-pound bodies to do the emergency lift. It can't be done without emotion. Emotions bring gain, but they can also bring blinding pain.

Once riding in old Baltimore
Heart-filled, head-filled with glee,
I saw a Baltimorean—keep looking straight at me.
Now I was eight and very small
And he was no whit bigger,
And so I smiled, but he poked out
His tongue, and called me "Nigger."
I saw the whole of Baltimore
From May until December;
Of all the things that happened there
That's all that I remember.
—Countee Cullen

The negative side of emotions is witnessed in despair. Neurobiological research illustrates how necessary hope is for survival. David Ingvar's research with Position Emission Tomography (PET Scan) shows computer-generated pictures of the neocortex during different states of mind. Ingvar's findings illustrate that the brain waves slow down measurably when people cannot anticipate a positive future. We cannot solve problems without hope.[3]

While negative emotions are responsible for a large percentage of job dysfunction, positive feelings are not a cure-all for every situation. In the 1930s, an Oklahoma high school football team could not win a game. Disappointed by the repeated defeats, a local oilman promised every coach and player a new car if they won their next game. The coaches and players ate, slept, and dreamt of defeating their opposition and getting new cars. The coaches gave their usual pregame pep talk and, as usual, the kids didn't listen. With a whoop and a holler, they ran onto the field to meet their opposition—and lost thirty-eight to nothing. Positive feelings, without the necessary skills, will not win the day.

THE NEED FOR SELF-CONTROL

In the effective listener, indeed the effective person, emotions must always be subject to the faculties of reason and will. Difficulties and stress occur in everyone's life on earth. Like the weather, circumstances change and this causes a change in feelings. You never know what the next day or night holds for you. Without the checks and balances of reason and will, you could be on a perpetual, emotional roller coaster.

Bill and Tom were drinking coffee at an all-night cafe. They had a lengthy discussion about the difference between irritation, anger, and rage. At about 1:00 A.M., Bill said, "Look, Tom, I'll show you an example of irritation." He went to the pay telephone, put in a coin, and dialed a number at random. The phone rang and rang and rang. Finally a sleepy voice at the other end answered. "I'd like to speak to Jones," Bill said. "There's no one here named Jones," the disgruntled man replied as he hung up. "That," Bill said to Tom, "is an irritated man."

An hour later, at 2:00 A.M., Bill said, "Now I'll show you an angry man. He went to the phone again, dialed the same number, and let it ring. Eventually the same sleepy voice answered the phone. Bill asked, "May I please speak with Jones?" The angry reply was a bit louder than before, "There's no one here named Jones." This time the man slammed down the receiver.

An hour later, at 3:00 A.M., Bill said, "Now, Tom, I'll show you an example of rage." He went to the phone, dialed the same number, and let it ring. When the sleepy man finally answered, Bill said, "Hi, this is Jones. Have there been any calls for me?" You can imagine how the man felt. We are all emotionally manipulated, to some degree, by people in our environment. The result is frequently a lower self-image and negative self-talk.

We are almost always engaged in a subconscious monologue with ourselves. Unfortunately, almost three-quarters of this self-talk is negative. The subconscious mind believes whatever we tell it; it will make the external reality conform to the internal image. Biochemical changes occur in the body in response to emotional input in the mind. These biochemical changes precipitate intense feelings that are impossible to ignore. Consequently, our inner speech influences behavior, feelings, sense of self-esteem, and ultimately, how we listen. It's easier to act yourself into a better way of feeling than it is to feel your way into a better way of acting.

You can change your self-talk and program positive outcomes in conversations with difficult people.

Bernice works in a tough business with a lot of stress, compounded by a personality conflict with one of her colleagues. This associate seems to take pleasure in making her life difficult. She tenses up and becomes defensive when this person is present. She is not able to constructively criticize and make pertinent requests from this individual who reports to her.

After identifying the need for emotional control, Bernice practiced relaxation techniques and visualization of control privately. She was able to transfer her visualization in private to performance in public, and it saved her job.

THE HAZARD OF UNRECOGNIZED FEELINGS

Emotions that you're unaware of are like lions on the loose ready to spring on you when you least expect them. It's dangerous not to know what you're feeling. You are not in a position to control your emotions until you have identified them. As a matter-of-fact, the only way to control your emotions is to identify those people, subjects, and words that trigger them, and to practice self-control. First practice in your imagination and then in the actual setting with the person, subject, or terminology. Don't put yourself under undue stress. The more you are able to practice self-control in emotional situations, the more control you will gain over your life.

Extinguishing behavior that hinders you will not extinguish your feelings. You will still have your emotions of like or dislike, but you will have control. Your goal is to extinguish the emotional response that occurs when you are not in control. Slamming down a book or a receiver, staring, raising your voice, turning away, and being absolutely silent are emotional responses that end communication. When these overreactions are extinct, you will have control of your emotions rather than having them control you. Practice makes perfect. Identify your emotional triggers and practice emotional control.

The skill of extinction is used to achieve weight loss. Having predetermined that you will not eat a hot fudge sundae, you approach it, look at it, outstare it, turn it around, smell it, and then push it away. The more you practice this behavior, the more successful you will be at extinguishing old behavior.

You will cease imbibing things that are not profitable to you and begin developing new neuropatterns in your brain, resulting in new habits. Practice the skill of extinction by identifying who and what touches your emotions, either positively or negatively, and then *practice control.* To recognize your own self-talk and discover your feelings about the people, subjects, and language around you, relax and listen to your thoughts. Deep breathing helps you relax.

Generate positive emotions. Certain actions, such as aerobic exercise, will generate positive emotions. Get your heart rate up to about 70 percent capacity for fifteen or twenty minutes. Use what music therapists call the "isomodic principle." Match music to your somber mood and then gradually change the music to an upbeat mood. Stimulate the brain's production of serotonin, a neurotransmitter responsible for making you feel calm and relaxed, by eating about 1 1/2 ounces of carbohydrates such as popcorn or pretzels. Sit under a "full-spectrum fluorescent" light, get a good night's sleep, meditate, pray, and think positively. This technique will help you control your emotions.

THREE AREAS FOR EMOTIONAL CONTROL

An effective listener knows how to control his or her emotions in at least three areas: (1) with speakers, regardless of who they are, (2) with subject matter, regardless of what it is, and (3) with language or words that are used, regardless of what they are.[4]

The Speaker

If you are positive toward an individual, you tend not to listen effectively. Because of your positive attitude toward the speaker, you buy everything he or she says without evaluating the message. When you are negative toward the speaker, your response is equally nonobjective on the opposite end of the scale. The tendency is to turn off the speaker before he or she is finished making a case.

This predetermined judgment suggests that certain people have nothing worthwhile to say. Isn't it possible that even though you may not like a person, he or she may have insight or help that will be very important to you? You don't know the man who discovered penicillin. You may not even like him, but you have benefited from what he did. Realizing that people don't have to think or be like you to be effective and profitable is liberating. The "kiss of death" for the professional is not being able to get along with others! Can you afford not to control your emotions?

Emotional control is not neutrality. Neutrality is not necessarily a blessing. If you're neutral and not emotionally involved enough to care about a person or issue, you tend to go to sleep. Identify your emotions toward the significant people in your life. You may even want to log the initials of the people who come into your life during the next thirty days. Put a plus, a minus, or a zero by the person's name. (Keep your log where no one will find it! The people in your life may not have learned the value of emotional control yet!)

The Subject Matter

What issues or subjects touch your emotions? Do you feel positive, neutral, or negative about the following media issues?

Gun Control
Women in Combat
Computerized Dating
Equal Rights Amendment
Capital Punishment
Socialized Medicine

Organized Religion
Taxes
Pro-Choice or Right-To-Life
Inflation
Foreign Ownership of United States Property

What personal interest or experience predisposes you to positive or negative feelings on certain issues? Is retirement an emotional issue for you? Is job security, a promotion, or a performance appraisal an emotional issue? What are the emotional issues in your life? Can you control your emotions when you hear people discussing these issues?

In college debates students are taught to make a cogent presentation of an issue regardless of their personal prejudices and biases. Debaters must be prepared to discuss the pros and cons of a given issue. Just minutes before the debate begins, they are told which side they will argue. Whether presenting for or against the issue, success depends on having accurate information, interpreting it correctly, and responding appropriately, regardless of the debater's personal feelings about the issue. Examining all sides of an issue in the privacy of your own mind will be a helpful way to practice emotional control.

The Language

Certain terms elicit feelings of warmth and comfort, anger, or fear. What terms touch your emotions? What words do you respond to positively and negatively?

Speeding up Bear Mountain late at night on the empty, curving road was fun. But when he approached the last turn at the top, another car was careening toward him. He swerved just in time to avoid a collision, and as the cars passed, a lady yelled, "Pig." Angrily, he stuck his head out the window and yelled back, "Sow!" Satisfied with his retort he stepped on the gas, rounded the turn, and ran into a pig.

What terms touch your emotions in a negative way? How do you respond to the following words?

Republican
Jock
Sex
Intellectual
Democrat
Liberal
Conservative
Pig
Honkie
Bastard
Strike
Discrimination
Kike
Bitch
Management
Labor

Social psychologists have known about the dramatic impact that words have on your emotions and actions. Even the most educated people can be controlled. "Dr. Fox" received a tremendous ovation for his lecture at a medical convention, yet his presentation was devoid of any accurate medical content. He created bogus terms that sounded scientific, and used enough scientific terms with great positive emotional content to convince the conventioneers of his validity. He was an actor, not a doctor. Terms loaded with positive, emotional content give a halo effect to everything the speaker says, unless the listener is skilled to recognize and appropriately deal with this effect.

Do you know what words touch your emotions? Can you control your response when either positive or negative impact words are spoken in your presence? Practice will help you maintain control.

EMOTIONAL CONTROL EXERCISE Think about the five people that you have targeted to improve your communication with, write down their initials, and answer these questions:
1. _____2. _____3. _____4. _____5. _____
Are you positive, negative, or neutral towards these people? Place a plus (+), minus (−), or neutral (0) sign by the initials above.

What subjects do these people like to talk about? Write down one or two subjects on the line with the same number as their initials. Then, place the positive, neutral, or negative sign by the subject.

1. _____
2. _____
3. _____
4. _____
5. _____

What terms do these people like to use when communicating with you? Do you feel positive, neutral, or negative about the terms? Write down terms for each person and note your feelings by using one of the three signs.

1. _____
2. _____
3. _____

4. _____
5. _____

Now extend your thinking beyond the five people above and write down the initials, the subjects, and the language or terms that elicit an emotional response from you. Place a positive, neutral, or negative sign by each.

Initials of people who elicit an emotional response: _____

Subjects that elicit an emotional response: _____

Language or terms that elicit an emotional response: _____

Emotional reactions to speakers, topics, and language are directly related to your filtering agents. Defer judgment until you can respond rationally. Listen to the entire message before you respond. Empathize, identify with the speaker, and try to see things through his or her eyes while you listen. Keep your personal feelings in perspective. Tell somebody what you learned. Listen for something that will benefit you.

Effective listening involves emotional control. When you don't control your emotions, you lose the opportunity to understand and profit from the communication. I live between Maryknoll Seminary and Sing Sing Prison. It helps to bring balance to my life.

A local seminary used to loan horses to needy travelers. One day a man asked to borrow a horse. The priest offered a spirited horse, but warned that the horse responded only to religious language. The rider must use the appropriate words. "If you want the horse to walk, say, 'Thank God.' If you want the horse to canter, say, 'Thank God, thank God.' And, if you want the horse to gallop, say, 'Thank

God, thank God, thank God.' To make the horse stop, say 'Amen.'"

Off went the rider traveling at a gallop. He was making good time, but, unfortunately, he made a wrong turn and headed toward a cliff with a fifty-foot drop to rocks and water. He pulled on the reins in terror and tried to remember the words to stop the horse. Scared and frustrated, he closed his eyes resigning himself to fate. When he gave up, he relaxed and remembered the word in the nick of time. "Amen," he said with gusto. As the horse skidded to a stop at the edge of the cliff, the man looking down at the rocks and water uttered in great relief, "Thank God."

Remember to control your emotions! A trained listener is better able to relax in emotionally laden situations.

If you chart your emotions over a period of 30 days, you will notice that you tend to move toward the neutral zone. You are not locked into your habitual pattern or emotional response. This is a very liberating thought. We are in process and hold the keys to positive change.

EMOTIONAL CONTROL UNDER FIRE: "VERBAL SELF-DEFENSE"

*The way of a fool seems right to him, but a
wise man listens to advice.*
—King Solomon

*He who ignores discipline despises himself, but
whoever heeds correction gains understanding.*
—King Solomon

THE LANGUAGE OF EFFECTIVE LISTENING

Reckless words pierce like a sword, but the
tongue of the wise brings healing.
—King Solomon

A word fitly spoken is like apples of gold in a
setting of silver.—King David

You need emotional control when you are being criticized. Not all criticism is negative, but all criticism is judgmental and can be manipulative. From its Latin root *criticus* comes the concept of a neutral, objective appraisal of ideas and actions. Criticism, if used properly, encourages and enhances personal growth and relationships. If criticism is used correctly, it will motivate people, encourage self-improvement, and teach and communicate needs and desires. If criticism is used incorrectly, it can destroy self-esteem, initiative, growth, and responsibility. This is especially true of negative criticism.

Perhaps you have heard statements similar to these. "Come on, John. You've been around here for five years. You know better than *that*." Or, "Are you kidding? That idea is as old as the ages. I thought you had something new."

How would you react to positive statements such as these? "Wow, John. You've only been here a few days and you've already got the idea of how to do it!" Or, "That's a great idea. I'm glad to hear something new."

Why is the response to negative criticism often anger, frustration, or depression? Why is it difficult to respond effectively and constructively to negative criticism? It's not uncommon for the person who is being criticized to respond with verbal or physical abuse. Even positive criticism can come across negatively. Sometimes it feels like condescension or manipulation. Or, perhaps it is insincere flattery. Are you satisfied with the way you respond to positive criticism of your work?

Figure 7.1. Effective listeners control their emotions
even when others lose theirs.

Both positive and negative criticism can be handled in the
same manner. You need to reorient your thinking to the nature
of the criticism. Shift the spotlight of negative criticism from
yourself to the true issue. This is a critical evaluation and
response skill. How you evaluate and respond will influence
your self-esteem and your future.

Oil filters, coffee filters, and air filters—the world is full of
filters to eliminate impurities and distortions. The same principle applies to words. Use the appropriate "filters" to evaluate
and respond to the message. You wouldn't pour coffee
grounds into a cup and add water. Why would you allow all of
the information thrown at you to enter without filters?

THE COMMUNICATION STYLE FILTER

Virginia Satir identified five distinct styles or patterns of language behavior that people use under stress. These styles can also be used to learn how people criticize. Dr. Suzette Haden Elgin has done a masterful job of interpreting Satir and conveys her concepts in a series of books on *The Gentle Art of Verbal Self-Defense.* If you can understand and identify these styles, you have the first filter to screen both positive and negative criticism. The style filter will help you profit from constructive criticism and protect you from negative criticism.

The Placater

The Placater is fearful that others will become angry and cut him or her off from personal interaction. In the movie *Marty,* Ernest Borgnine plays Marty, and he and his buddy are in a bar trying to decide what to do that night.

> Marty: "What do you want to do tonight?"
> Friend: "Oh, I don't know. What do you want to do?"
> Marty: "I don't care. What do you think?"

The ineffective conversation continues with each afraid of hurting the other and, eventually, losing the friendship.

When criticizing, the Placater has difficulty telling the flat, naked truth. He or she is more concerned about how the other person will feel towards him or her than in getting the point across.

The Blamer

The Blamer feels powerless and thinks that no one cares about him or her. To compensate, the Blamer tries to take charge and show who's the boss. When criticizing, the Blamer tends to exaggerate statements to make sure that the point is made.

"You're always *overspending* your budget."
"You *never* do things right."

The Computer

The Computer is afraid to disclose his or her feelings. A good example of a Computer is Mr. Spock on "Star Trek." When criticizing, the Computer blocks out all emotion from his or her voice.

"Without question, the job can be done in a different way."

"People can logically conclude that the solution lies in adopting the new policy."

The Distracter

The Distracter does not maintain any of the patterns. Instead, he or she shifts from Computer to Blamer to Placater. He or she feels compelled to say something and say it right now! But since the Distracter doesn't know what to say, incoherent thoughts follow.

"The bill *could* have been paid on time, don't you think? Well *maybe* not, but it's always being paid late. Anyway, a rational person would be very concerned."

When criticizing, the Distracter hits you with a diverse set of feelings simultaneously. You have to sift through the Distracter's criticism to get to the element of truth, if there is one.

The Leveler

The Leveler tells it like it is. When the Leveler is sincere, he or she is using the most helpful of the communicating styles. Tom Dunkerton, a retired senior vice-president at Saatchi, Saatchi, and Compton Advertising, is one of the best "Levelers" I know. I have observed how being direct can save hours of business meetings.

"Three times out of the last eight you requested documentary support for our statistics. On each occasion you found our work accurate. We are not dealing with a critical matter here. Why not let it go *this* time? Your request will slow us up and we won't meet our deadline."

This is not a verbal attack; it is a thoughtful request. Sometimes you assume the Leveler is the enemy, and the "nice guy" upstairs is your supporter. The truth may be just the opposite.

The following examples show the five styles being used in a "crisis" situation. Five people are trapped in an elevator stuck between the sixth and seventh floors.[5]

> Placater: "Oh, I *hope* I didn't do anything to cause this. I sure didn't *mean* to."
>
> Blamer: "Which one of you idiots was fooling around with the buttons?"
>
> Computer: "There is undoubtedly some perfectly logical reason why this elevator isn't moving. Certainly there is no cause whatever for alarm."
>
> Distracter: "Did one of you hit the stop button? Oh, I didn't *mean* that; of course, none of you would do anything like that. It is, however, extremely easy to do that sort of thing by accident. *Why* do things like this only happen to me?"
>
> Leveler: "Personally, I'm scared."

When you aren't sure how to respond to criticism, use the Computer style. Control your emotions and be as objective as possible. Then, as you gain equilibrium, synchronize with the speaker. Recognizing the different styles gives you greater objectivity in evaluating the criticism and helps you decide whether or not you need more information. You can decide how best to respond.

A COMMUNICATION STYLE EXERCISE Write down the initials of the five people with whom you are going to build your relationship over the next thirty days. Try to identify the usual styles he or she uses when criticizing: Placater, Blamer, Computer, Distracter, or Leveler.

Initials _____ Style _____

Initials _____ Style _____

Initials _____ Style _____

Initials _____ Style _____

Initials _____ Style _____

THE TRUTH FILTER

If feedback has any validity, find the valid point. Feedback may contain only one "kernel" amidst a bushel of chaff. Look for it, then admit to the valid point, and sincerely thank the critic for the information.

This process accomplishes four purposes. You establish that you are a reasonable person. You let the criticizer focus on the point you agree on, and forget the overstatement. You protect your self-esteem and the esteem of the criticizer. You may gain valuable insight. The perspective of others will help you become all you can be! "Listen to advice and accept instruction, and, in the end, you will be wise."

> Critic: "You are *always* late."
>
> Response: "Bill, I was late *today,* but that won't happen again."

THE EMOTION FILTER

Separate the criticism from the criticizer! Emotional criticism may have roots in the criticizer's emotional needs. His own needs, hurts, or fears may cause him to attack before assessing the timing or appropriateness of the criticism. The emotion filter lets you consider the source and determine the appropriateness. Do you have control over the point being

THE LANGUAGE OF EFFECTIVE LISTENING

criticized, or is a distraught criticizer looking for a place to put responsibility? As you run the speaker's words through the emotion filter, you shift the spotlight from yourself to the speaker. Now you are an observer, not a victim.

Since the spotlight is shifted from you to the speaker, and emotional baggage is stripped from the speaker's words, you can deal with the message. However, even without emotion, a message can be slanted. You need another filter.

THE PERSUASIVE TECHNIQUES FILTER

Isolate any part of the message that uses persuasive techniques and resist them long enough to ask relevant questions. Your best defense is to follow the advice, "know yourself!" Which of the following techniques would most likely influence you?[6]

Bandwagon: "Everybody's doing it! Get on the bandwagon with us."

Card stacking: Using illustrations, facts, or opinions that have been carefully selected to make the best or worst possible case for an idea, product, or person. The speaker presents only information that strengthens his point, and omits anything that may give you another point of view. "Pearly White toothpaste will whiten your teeth and freshen your breath. Your children will love it." What you haven't been told is that the sweetener in "Pearly White" will shorten your life.

Glittering generality: "Virtue" words like democracy, justice, or motherhood are associated with the ideas or products being promoted. "Our decision is based upon democratic principles and is a kinder approach to the problem."

Name calling: Labels are used to bait the listener into condemning something or someone without evidence.

Without any consideration of the ethics involved, a reputation can quickly and easily be destroyed. "Yeah, George got that promotion, but the boss doesn't know that he is a cheater."

Plain folks: This technique associates an idea or product with the common man who is "just like you." The guy next door is assumed to have the same values as you. For example, "I notice that XYZ company has installed a BQ computer system. They are in the same business as you, and *they* are very happy with the results."

Testimonial: A highly accepted individual or group is associated with an idea or product to influence its acceptance. "The president of this country's most successful corporation uses this system." A disliked individual or group is associated with an idea or product to influence its rejection.

A very wealthy plantation owner wanted to find the best possible husband for his stunningly beautiful daughter. He sent letters to eligible bachelors across the southeast declaring that the man who passed a certain test would marry his daughter and inherit all his wealth. On the appointed day, dozens of eager, young men congregated in his home.

"The thing I admire most in a man is courage and a strong desire to overcome all obstacles." He took the men to his Olympic-sized swimming pool stocked with sharks, electric eels, stingrays, alligators, and water moccasins. "The first man who successfully swims the length of my pool will have the incomparable privilege of marrying my beautiful daughter, Lulubelle, and inheriting my enormous estate."

Almost instantly, a splash was heard at the far end of the pool. A human form skimmed through the water faster than you would think possible. A daring, young man raced through the water, reached the other end of the pool, and leaped out as a dozen jaws snapped behind him. There was a moment of stunned silence followed by a roar of applause.

"Son, I've never seen such an instantaneous display of courage in my life. I'm proud to have you marry my daughter and inherit my property. Come on in and I'll introduce you to Lulubelle and show you my papers."

"Sir, I'll be glad to do that, but first, just give me five minutes with the guy who pushed me into that pool!"

Circumstances can be a most effective persuader.

THE PERSPECTIVE FILTER

Determine the false assumption. If you believe an invalid assumption is inherent in the criticism, identify and reject the false assumption.

> Critic: "If you had been *early,* the project would have been approved."
>
> Response: "I don't believe that the entire project rests upon the *time* of my arrival."

Balance the criticism against everything you have accomplished in your life. The scales have to weigh in your favor.

> Critic: "Harry, you *really* missed the boat on this one."
>
> Response: "Hey, *nobody* bats a thousand, not even the boss. We'll get 'em *next* time."

"Fine," you might be thinking about all these filters. "That has got to be the Rube Goldberg of the thought world. By the time I run the message through all these filters, my criticizer will be long gone."[7]

This can happen, especially when someone gives you a quick shot and leaves. You're left hanging high and dry with no defense or resolution. What can you do when you are unable to give an immediate response to criticism? Determine the appropriate filter, then mentally review an appropriate response. This mental exercise will prepare you for an encounter you can respond to verbally. With a little practice, you will be able to run messages through your filters almost instantly and be ready to respond.

The four immediate responses to negative criticism listed below can be used with discretion. Your voice "quality" will be important. Voice quality includes pitch, nasality, volume, breathiness, harshness, and timbre. Albert Mehrabian and other highly respected researchers discovered that 38 percent of the meaning of what we say is not in the words, but in how we say them. The work of Manfred Clynes as reported by Suzette Haden Elgin demonstrates that "intonation that leaps sharply up and down in pitch, that cuts words off choppily, that punches at certain words and phrases, that clings to a straight monotonous line. . . " are linear and angular rather than curved, and communicate negative emotions. Positive emotions, which are more likely to illicit a positive response, are expressed by smooth, curving intonation.[8]

1. Short-circuit the message.

> Critic (Manager bursts into your office): "Where are those reports? Aren't you finished yet?"

Response (Smiling): "Good morning, Sam. How are you?"

Critic: "Huh? Oh, good morning."

2. Communicate your feelings.

Critic (Calmly): "You're not helping me. You're making me nervous. Please leave me alone, and I'll be finished."

3. Put yourself in his or her place.

Response: "Sam, I know this is important. You can help me by making sure that no one disturbs me and by making sure the copy machine is free."

4. Ask for more information. There may be numerous reasons why your work has been criticized. The initial point of criticism may be insufficient for you to profit from. If additional information will help you, ask for it. This is the easiest and safest quick response to use. It gives both you and the critic a chance to gain equilibrium, and it gives you a chance to gain control of your emotions.

Critic: "Your report did not satisfy the requirement."

Response: "Bill, which of the requirements are you referring to?"

To profit and protect yourself from criticism, you need a strategy for long-term response. Determine the importance of the criticism. Does it warrant your attention? Weigh the pros and cons of change. If you want to take action on it, ask yourself how much energy you must invest. Plan to make the necessary changes. The following four strategies will help you.

1. Make a written contract with yourself. State in writing what you are going to do and when you will do it. Sign your name just as if you were signing a contract. Make sure that the behavior you describe is something you can and will do. Furthermore, your behavior should be, at least in the beginning, consistent with your commitment.

2. Decide what changes must be made. What elements or factors are involved in the change? Break down the elements necessary to effect change into manageable tasks. For example, if you want to improve your voice quality when responding to criticism, practice your response with a tape recorder. Imagine yourself appropriately responding to criticism and record your response. Listen to the tape and evaluate your voice. Are the intonations smooth and positive? Think about how you can improve your response, and record the appropriate changes. When you think you have perfected your response on tape, play it for a few friends, ask for their evaluation, and then make any necessary changes. When you have perfected your response on tape, repeat it with the recording until it seems natural to you. In the long run, this procedure will help you appropriately respond in emotionally volatile situations.

3. Build some penalties into your practices or procedures that will flag you down; or create some distances that make it difficult to continue with the criticized behavior. For example, our workshop participants ask five colleagues to inform them if they are or are not doing what they have contracted to do. People would rather be told they are doing right. By putting themselves "on the spot" the participants try harder and are often more successful.

4. Think of the reward you will gain by changing your behavior. You may become a model of maturity for others in

Figure 7.2. Effective listeners profit from constructive criticism.

your group. You could positively influence an entire work group. You will become more highly esteemed by your colleagues. Make no mistake, your success is highly correlated to how your associates perceive you. Colleagues will be more inclined to trust you and tell you what they *really* think about other matters.

How can I respond to criticism so that both the criticizer and I profit, and our relationship grows? More important than set rules or formulas is the spirit in which criticism is offered and accepted. Criticism can be a positive form of emotional support, and a step towards growth, productivity, satisfaction, and fulfillment. You will be criticized the rest of your life. No one enjoys criticism, but it is a vital tool for personal growth. The effective listener learns how to profit from it.

Emotions, like fire, can burn or warm. You decide if you will be warmed or burned by choosing how you will respond. You may have been burned by painful experiences and words. You may have been singed by untimely or inappropriate feelings. You can try to bury your emotions, but you can't extinguish the coals, and they flare up when least expected. When fire is under control it is a valuable friend. You will never be without emotions that can warm or burn. Learn emotional control and your emotions will be a source of strength to you.

E I G H T

Communisuasion: How to Listen Persuasively

It is almost impossible to change a person's belief system or preferences without that person's permission!—*A.K. Robertson*

We are so resistant to anything that might disrupt our belief systems, our picture of the world, that we will unconsciously seek and allow ourselves to be drawn only to those views that we agree with.—*J.A.C. Brown*

ontrary to popular belief, it is the effective listener, not the speaker, who often controls the conversation. Listening can be a powerful persuasion technique. Every emotion and every thought seek a companion. The need for communion is so strong that the speaker will often bond with the listener who provides companionship, and follow the leading question or probing response. By asking the appropriate questions and responding in a manner that reflects the thoughts, feelings, and mannerisms of the speaker, the listener can often steer the thoughts of the speaker. To be an effective "persuader," the listener must first prove himself or herself trustworthy.

My associate, Dr. Don Osgood, and I coined a word and created a workshop to explain, illustrate, and teach these concepts. The word *communisuasion* (TM) is composed of two words, *communis* which means understanding and *suasion* which means to influence with integrity. The effective listener is familiar with "communisuasion," which means to understand the client and influence with integrity.

BUILD TRUST

Trustworthiness is invaluable to a person's overall success. A twenty-year study conducted at Harvard University by Dr. Robert Coles established that the best way to ensure the success of your children is to teach them high moral values. The Forum Corporation researchers chose 341 salespeople from eleven companies, representing five different industries. One hundred seventy-three were high-performance professionals. One hundred sixty-eight were moderate producers. The salespeople had equal knowledge and ability. What separated the high performers from the moderate ones? Trust was the difference. The high performers were the most trustworthy.

Donald Seibert, former chief executive officer and chairman of the board of J.C. Penney Company, Inc., says, "Among the people I know at the top of the nation's major corporations, the personal quality that is regarded most highly is a solid, unwavering sense of integrity. The higher a person moves up in business, the more important it is for his peers and superiors to feel they can depend on his word. They have to know that he's a 'straight shooter' in every sense of the word, one who won't cut moral corners to further his own interests."

Senior managers agreed that after "concern for results," the most important trait that enhances executive success is "integrity." More than 66 percent of the salespeople questioned listed this quality as a key executive characteristic.[1]

Fred Clarkson's Boston challenge provides a homey illustration of the value of trust. Fred claimed that he could sell more five-dollar bills for ten dollars than traditional salesmen could sell ten-dollar bills for five dollars. Each man was allowed twenty attempts. That evening, on the streets of Boston, Fred sold six five-dollar bills for ten dollars while his competition sold only two ten-dollar bills for five dollars. The six buyers who obviously made poor purchases were asked why they bought five-dollar bills for ten dollars. All six said they knew it was a poor trade, but something inside of them said it was the right thing to do. Eighteen people refused to pay five dollars for a ten-dollar bill. When they were asked why they passed up such a good deal, the nonbuyers admitted that it was an excellent trade, but they opposed the salespeoples' manipulative techniques.[2]

You may be convinced that the listener's response to the speaker will determine the speaker's response to the listener, but it may be difficult to act on this belief in real life. When the speaker's characteristics, subject matter, or emotionally laden words are distasteful, it is difficult to be nonjudgmental. You can distance yourself from the speaker with your nonverbal responses.

To assure the speaker you are trustworthy requires flexibility. The less you have in common with the persuadee, the more flexible you need to be to gain his or her trust. The more you have in common with the persuadee, the greater the likelihood you will be trusted. We tend to trust people who are like us.

GAIN RAPPORT
When you don't have rapport, tension is increased. You need to consciously *identify* the unique behavior patterns of the person you want to influence. When you have consciously identified his or her characteristics, and you are flexible and *reflect* this pattern to the speaker, tension is reduced. The

speaker is more likely to accept your suggestions in a relaxed atmosphere. When properly applied, the reflection technique builds trust and gives you the opportunity to prove yourself. It is not necessary, and it may be dangerous, to mirror the speaker. Research indicates that top salespeople establish similar postures and gestures as their customers and clients, but they do not mirror them.[3] People are most comfortable with, and most open to, those who are like themselves. If you are different, you are often suspected! When you are trusted, you can *suggest* ideas or products to the speaker, and you have a high probability for success. You don't want to sell an idea or product that is either inappropriate or against your "client's" will. If you do, the sale will come back to haunt you. When you have effectively listened to the speaker you are better able to powerfully influence his or her decision. Effective selling is completely customer-centered.

"To communicate on the level of real persuasion—not the seductive, deceptive, or manipulative persuasion forms. . . requires a fuller appreciation of the other's values, views, priorities, basic beliefs, and goals. Persuasion is a coactive process in which both profit. There must be a benefit to both the persuader and the persuadee."[4]

Product knowledge, although important, is not the key to sales. It is important to know why and how the product was created, its benefits and advantages, how it compares to the competition, how it operates, and how the buyer can save time, money, or both. This knowledge is only about 20 percent of what is needed. "Eighty percent of the knowledge prerequisite to effective sales is about human behavior, particularly the behavior of your client."[5]

In order for persuasion to be effective and a "coactive process in which both profit," the persuader needs to understand the persuadee's needs, mannerisms, motives, and patterns of behavior. He or she needs to sincerely reflect the speaker's thoughts, feelings, and mannerisms, and then suggest how his or her idea meets the persuadee's needs. The process is:

- I dentify
- R eflect
- S uggest

Understanding the persuadee is significantly enhanced when the persuader encourages the persuadee to talk. Talking is easily encouraged by asking timely, probing questions. Questions are used to identify the persuadee's styles and needs. As the persuadee shares information, the informed listener IDENTIFIES the following categories or patterns of behavior.

1. The Speaker's Body Language
2. The Speaker's Primary Motivation
3. The Speaker's Sorting Pattern
4. The Speaker's Preferred Sensory Mode

IDENTIFY THE SPEAKER'S BODY LANGUAGE

A lot of nonsense has been written about body language and it has convinced some readers that they can become instant experts and omnipotent persuaders after perusing a few popular paperback books. Nonverbal communication is more than body language. An in-depth study of nonverbal communication has revealed hundreds of thousands of different ways the body speaks, necessitating a new vocabulary to describe the findings. The following terms are used to describe body language.

"Proxemics," the study of space and how people use and relate to it

"Paralinguists," the study of all cues in oral speech other than the content of the words spoken

"Allokines," the smallest units of analysis of body movements

"Allophones," the smallest units of analysis of human speech

Nonverbal communication includes the study of "posture and facial expressions, but many other things as well. [It includes]. . . the inflection and quality of the voice, the distance between speakers and listeners, the messages conveyed by the way a speaker chooses to clothe or decorate the body, the method a speaker uses to decide when it is his or her turn to talk, and so on."[6]

Nonverbal communication will be discussed in greater detail in chapter 9. Listeners should be aware of the following key areas.

Elements of "Body Language"

You should be aware of all changes in body language. Albert Mehrabian says that the body projects the thoughts and feelings of the mind, and will visibly convey about 55 percent of the speaker's meaning. As Sigmund Freud said, "He that has eyes to see and ears to hear may convince himself that no mortal may keep a secret. If his lips are silent, he chatters with his fingertips; betrayal oozes out of him at every pore."[7]

THE SPEAKER'S VOICE The way words are spoken, Mehrabian concluded, gives you about 37 percent of the meaning that is being conveyed. Is the voice harsh, soft, loud, or nasal? What is the volume, rate, and pitch? You will not mirror distasteful elements, but it is helpful to be aware of offensive elements and notice if they are constant or intermittent.

THE SPEAKER'S FACIAL EXPRESSION The face reveals a significant amount of the speaker's attitudes and feelings. Meaning is read in the face. (See chapter 9.) Poker players practice maintaining the same facial expression throughout the game. They wear "poker faces" to conceal the true quality of their poker hands.

THE SPEAKER'S EYES Eyes have been called the "windows of the soul." We are aware of communication coming from the eyes. "If looks could kill, he'd be dead," is an example of such a message. It is difficult for most speakers in our culture to control their eyes and hide their attitude. Observe the direction of eye movements. Are they moving up, down, or to the side? Are the eyes focused toward you or away from you? Does the person look up frequently; is he or she very optimistic? Increased eye contact among Anglo-Saxons usually means increased comfort and trust. On the other hand, many Latins and other cultures consider increased eye contact rude.

THE SPEAKER'S PROXEMIC ZONE How close does the speaker want to be to you? In North America, about four feet or more is usually a comfortable business distance. If the listener is too close or too far away, the speaker is uncomfortable but usually doesn't know why. Notice whether or not the speaker wants you to be closer or farther away. We may violate proxemics by missing the speaker's preference.

VERBAL PROXEMICS The listener can also be too close or too far away verbally. Be aware of how formal or informal your language should be. "Familiarity breeds contempt." Let the speaker set the pace and don't intrude on the speaker's mental space.

CONTACT OR NO CONTACT Some speakers prefer to touch or pat a listener. Is it a friendly touch toward an associate or a stiff, pointed finger toward an antagonist? Others prefer no physical contact. Be aware of the speaker's preference.

TERRITORIAL RIGHTS The speaker will identify with certain objects and specific locations. Observe his or her degree of possessiveness regarding the office, a pen, a pencil, etc.

THE SPEAKER'S BODY STANCE Observe the speaker's posture. Is he or she sitting or standing, rigid or relaxed, leaning forward or back, demonstrating reluctance, displaying interest and involvement, or positioned back and away?

THE SPEAKER'S GESTURES How often does the speaker gesture? Are the gestures relaxed and confident or emphatic and concerned? Are they big and broad, demonstrating emotional involvement, or small and constrained, signaling the speaker to be careful of what he or she says?

RECOGNIZE THE SPEAKER'S PRIMARY MOTIVATION

At any given time, the speaker may have a primary or umbrella motivation under which all other motives dwell as subordinates. Some primary motivaters are productivity, power, and relationships.[8] You can discern the speaker's primary motivation by asking probing questions and listening astutely. A person motivated by *productivity* is driven by what he or she can accomplish or "make happen." A person motivated by *power* seeks personal autonomy or control over his or her circumstances, so that he or she has "ownership" over his or her job responsibilities and personal life. A person motivated by *relationships* is concerned about how others may feel, think, and react to his or her decisions. Listening carefully will provide this information. Can you identify the primary motivation of the people with whom you are improving communication?

IDENTIFY THE SPEAKER'S SORTING PATTERN

Everyone processes information in his or her own way and for his or her own purpose. At any given moment, an individual is consciously or unconsciously acquiring information to reach a goal, protect his or her position or possessions, or prevent failure. Listen intently. Is the speaker defensive, tentative, or confident about discussing the subject?

IDENTIFY THE SPEAKER'S PREFERRED SENSORY MODE

You can see, hear, feel, smell, and taste. John Grinder and Richard Bandler have demonstrated that you have a primary sense by which you prefer to learn and enjoy life. This sensory system is supported by the other modes. If you identify the speaker's preferred sensory system, you will understand him or her better. You can identify the speaker's sensory system by listening, not talking.

Sales experts claim that about 80 percent of the U.S. population prefers the "show me" system.[9] When we see it, we "get it." The next preferred system is hearing. Recently, more attention has been given to touch, taste, and smell. Taste and smell are less preferred systems than the first three. Taste and smell are often treated as a single system because, physiologically, they are closely connected.

We can identify the speaker's preferred sensory mode by listening to the words he or she uses. Examples of seeing phrases are: "I see what you mean." "That's clear." "The outlook is speculative." or, "I foresee." Seeing phrases are easy to recognize. Hearing phrases such as, "That rings a bell." "You are coming through loud and clear." "That sounds good to me." or, "We are in tune." are also easy to recognize. They are used most frequently by speakers who prefer to learn, understand, and live through the hearing mode.

Speakers who prefer the feeling or touching mode might say, "That is easy to grasp." "It's an uphill climb from here." "It flows well." or, "That's a hot idea."

Those who prefer the smelling mode might say, "That situation stinks." "He came out of it smelling like a rose." or, "Let's sniff around and see what we can find." Perfume testers have developed this sense. Nonsighted professionals in my workshops claimed to identify colleagues by smell. It is possible that when one sense is lost or diminished we rely more heavily upon the other senses. Interestingly, the sense of smell has the strongest memory component and can be used to recall situations that seemed beyond memory. In a flash, the smell of an object once familiar to us can catapult us back in time.

Speakers using the tasting mode might say, "That deal leaves a bad taste in my mouth." "I can almost taste victory now." or, "It was a real sweet shot." Wine tasters have developed this sense.

Every word will not fit into one of the five sensory modes. Words such as indicate, think, decide, and deliberate do not indicate a specific mode. If the speaker uses these words, you will want to respond in a similar mode. If you are uncertain of the speaker's mode, use one of the nonspecific words.

To heighten your awareness of the various sensory preferences, make a list of words you hear and place them in the various sensory categories. Discovering your preferred sensory category will also be insightful. The following exercise will help you.

Practice Identifying Your Preferred Sensory Mode

Whether you prefer a visual, auditory, or feeling-action mode is a matter of conditioning.[10] You can increase your level of awareness and determine if you have a preference by answering the two sets of questions. Perhaps neither of the options are what you would normally say. Just read the scenarios and choose the response most closely related to what you would say. Circle your choice and add up your totals. One choice is in the seeing mode, one in the hearing mode, one in the feeling/touching mode, and one does not use any of the sensory modes.

SET ONE

1. Your boss has called a meeting to determine if you think it would be fair for you to rearrange your vacation time to accommodate an overly demanding customer. The deal is unfair to you. You will be asked to express your opinion. What will you say?

   a. It's clear that it would be unfair for me to have to change my vacation plans at this time.
   b. It sounds like it would be unfair for me to have to change my vacation plans at this time.
   c. I feel that it would be unfair for me to have to change my vacation plans at this time.
   d. I don't think that it would be fair for me to have to change my vacation plans at this time.

2. The departmental planning session is going nowhere. You know that anymore time spent on it will be totally wasted. You want to say something, but you want to be diplomatic. What would you say?

   a. It isn't clear to me what's missing, but I believe we are overlooking some important points.
   b. I can't tell exactly what they are, but it sounds like some important points have been left unspoken.
   c. I don't have a grasp of what we need, but I feel we have the resources within this group to pull things together.
   d. It seems we are missing some key concepts that are necessary for a satisfactory resolution.

3. You recognize that you have made a serious mistake in judgment, and now you are being called "on the carpet" for it. How would you admit your mistake?

   a. You're right, it looks like I made a mistake on this one.
   b. You're right, it sounds like I made a mistake on this one.
   c. I feel you are right, I made a mistake on this one.
   d. You're right, I believe I made a mistake on this one.

4. You are trying to lose weight and have some success. Your associates disapprove of your diet. How would you respond to their criticism?

   a. You can see that the diet works. Take a look at the scale—seeing is believing.
   b. The diet speaks for itself. I lost ten pounds; it works.
   c. I feel much lighter and I don't get as tired as I used to. The diet works.

    d.   I think the point is obvious. The scale proves the diet is effective.

5. The rumor mill is disparaging the character of a colleague. You know the rumor is false. When an associate tells you the rumor, what would you say to set the record straight?

    a.   I have a different point of view. Take a look at the facts and you'll see that the rumor is false.
    b.   I have heard what really happened. Listen to the facts; the rumor is false.
    c.   I feel that I have the truth. When you get ahold of the facts, you'll know the rumor is false.
    d.   I know the facts in this case, and I believe you will judge the rumor false when you understand them.

SET TWO

1. You are going to learn a new job skill. Which of the following options would you choose?

    a.   Learn by listening to a tape with an instructor.
    b.   Learn by watching a videotape with an instructor.
    c.   Learn by "walking through" the instructions with an instructor.

2. You are going to choose a recreational activity. Which one would you choose?

    a.   One that primarily uses the eyes?
    b.   One that primarily uses the ears?
    c.   One that primarily uses the hands?

3. Close your eyes and think about the interior of the first car you owned. Now, if you were to describe the interior, how would you do it? What words help you remember it best?

    a. Words that describe how the dashboard looked?
    b. Words that describe how the seats felt?
    c. Words that describe how the radio sounded?

Practice Identifying the Speaker's Preferred Sensory Mode

Just as you can identify your preferred sensory mode in different situations, you can also identify the speaker's preferred sensory mode. You want to be flexible so you can switch from your preferred sensory mode to the speaker's preferred sensory mode, if they are different. The following exercises will help you.

1. Listen to radio and television interviews, and practice identifying the various sensory modes.
2. Watch movies and, again, practice identifying sensory modes.
3. Listen closely to family members and friends. Can you identify a preferred sensory mode?
4. Finally, practice identifying a co-worker's preferred sensory mode.

After a few weeks of consciously trying to identify sensory modes, you will begin to do it unconsciously.

REFLECTING AND PACING

When you have identified the speaker's body language, primary motivation, sorting pattern, and preferred sensory mode, you can reflect them back to the speaker. Reflect any manner-

Figure 8.1. Effective listeners are conscious of the
speaker's nonverbal communication.

ism, style, or characteristic that is not a negative idiosyncrasy.
For example, if the client crosses his or her arms, you may
subtly cross your feet. If the client is more concerned about
maintaining positive relationships with associates than with
increasing productivity, you will want to demonstrate how you
and your service or product can encourage positive relationships. The client may be more concerned about *not failing*
than about being successful, or vice versa. In turn, state how
your product or service will meet this need. When possible,
use words from the client's preferred sensory mode throughout the discussion. If possible, listen more than you talk! Try
to talk at the same rate, pitch, and volume as the client. Remember, everyone judges others by his or her own standard.
The more flexible you are, the more persuasive you will be.

By being more flexible in your approaches to others, and by being more aware of their patterns and reflecting them, you will be more successful.

To ensure your success, observe the following cautions.

1. If you already have rapport, keep it; don't change a thing. "Don't fix it if it ain't broken." *Do* cautiously reflect some of the speaker's nonverbal communication to gain rapport.
2. Try to reflect one mannerism or style at a time.
3. Reflect the speaker's posture, gesture, voice, or eye movements, but do not mimic the speaker. Don't give the speaker the impression that you are strange or that you are making fun of him or her. It is better to reflect a similar mannerism, than to risk offending the speaker with mimicry.
4. Practice with "training wheels" by watching talk shows or similar programs. Turn down the volume on your television to decipher what is being said based on the nonverbal communication. Choose one character and carefully practice reflecting his or her mannerisms.

Reflecting is "speaking the language" of the other person so that you are understood. If you've ever had problems communicating with another person, it was probably because you were not speaking "the same language" even though you may have used the same words. Milton Erickson coined the term "pacing" to refer to "meeting the other person where he or she is, reflecting what he or she knows or assumes to be true, or matching some part of his or her ongoing experience."[11]

When we have rapport, the process of reflecting or pacing is often done unconsciously. "In moments of great rapport, a remarkable pattern of nonverbal communication can develop. Two people will mirror each other's movements—dropping a hand or shifting their body at exactly the same time. This happens so quickly that, without videotape or film replay, one is unlikely to notice the mirroring. But managers can learn to watch for disruptions in this mirroring because they are dramatically obvious when they occur. . . . Instead of smooth mirroring, there will be a burst of movement, almost as if both are losing balance. Arms and legs may be thrust out, and the whole body posture changed, in order to regain balance."[12]

The ability to work well with others is the primary cause of job success. The prime cause of job failure is unsatisfactory relationships. Eighty percent of dismissals are caused by poor interpersonal relationships. "Of the people important to your success, 75 percent are very different from you. They use time differently, make decisions differently, prefer to relate in different ways, and have different styles of communicating. . . . To sum up, high interpersonal flexibility is now associated with business success, and probably will be an even more important factor in the coming years."[13]

"Style flex" is the temporary adjustment of one individual to another in order to understand each other and work more effectively together.[14] This flexibility can be attained without losing your integrity or naturalness. "Women are far better at observing body language and using it effectively than men are."[15] At the beginning of our training workshop, men were afraid they might lose their individuality by getting "in sync" with another person. But, understanding does not mean giving up one's individuality. Those with the greatest flexibility or "requisite variety" of responses will be the most successful.

The best salespeople reflect their clients without compromising their integrity. They are adaptable in disclosing various personality traits. The flexible man or woman will eventually find a small piece of common ground that invariably exists with another person. Inflexible people tend to "show only one or two aspects of themselves, no matter who they are with or what the situation demands. This rigid or inflexible person generally will not make it to the top in the highly demanding world of sales and management."[16]

"The more two individuals share movement or posture together, the greater the rapport between them. Such rapport contributes to a sense of acceptance, belonging, and well-being."[17] This synchronization is a powerful communicator at the subconscious level. A smile is a universal language, and so is reflecting or pacing the speaker. When two people are effectively communicating, their bodies show it; "an eyelid blinks or a finger curls in synchrony with a particular word, sound, or voice stress."[18]

This phenomenon is demonstrated in workshop videos of individuals participating in effective listening exercises. As participants gain rapport, they unconsciously swivel in their chairs, rock, scratch, blink, smile, and make countless other movements in synchrony. They are unaware that they are synchronizing! I watched a 200-pound, 6-foot, black man from New York City synchronize with a 100-pound, 5-foot, white woman from Georgia. In contrast, I have seen two men or two women of similar backgrounds in discord.

Reflect on the Past and the Present

It may be possible to reflect or pace by identifying some biographical similarities. If something in your past agrees with the speaker's past, share that similarity. Did you go to the same school or live in the same state? What similarity in your past "paces" with the past of the person you would like to influence? Does some conclusion or issue join you together? Is there something in the present you agree on. You can usually agree at least 20 percent with anybody.

Reflect the Speaker's Feelings

Recognize if the persuadee is sad, angry, surprised, fearful, disgusted, or happy, and reflect a similar emotion on your face and in your voice. For example, if a customer calls and is irate about a faulty product, late appointment, or improper charge, show your concern by also being irate, not about the customer, but about the error. By doing this, your customer will know that you understand how he or she feels. If your voice does not reflect concern similar to his or hers, the customer will become more irate. Do observe this caution: you don't have to accept culpability for the error at this point. You are merely establishing that a problem exists.

> Customer: "We asked that the product be delivered *next* month, and it's already here. Our warehouse is *overstocked* and you guys will want to bill us thirty days *ahead* of our schedule. *What* went wrong?
>
> Response: "That's terrible. You wanted the product *next* month, and it's already arrived at an *overstocked* warehouse, and the billing process is thirty days *ahead* of schedule. I'll speak with shipping and find out *what* went wrong and get back to you."

The problem has not been resolved, but the first appropriate step has been taken. Speak the language of his or her feelings. Matching the mood brings agreement; mismatching the mood brings disharmony, distance, and blurred understanding.

Reflect the Persuadee's Body Language

More than 700,000 nonverbal cues may be subconsciously shared in communication.[19] If we consciously pace recognizable mannerisms, the subconscious mannerisms follow. When interpreting body language, exercise caution in reading clusters. No single movement should be considered a definitive statement about the persuadee without other elements to back it up. For example, a man may have his arms crossed, a stance interpreted as closed-minded and defensive. However, he may be cold, tired, or have a sore arm, and not be defensive at all.

But, if the person has his arms crossed, tends to turn away from you, and continually shakes his head horizontally, you are not in rapport!

Reflect the Speaker's Breathing

In Japan, at the beginning of some Quality Circle meetings, all participants breathe in unison. This is more than a physical exercise; the unison breathing "establishes a climate of agreement and harmony. . . . Studies show that as these meetings get underway, the executives in attendance bypass small matters and concentrate on important issues."[20] The astute listener can often observe the heaving chest, the rise and fall of the shoulders, or the stomach of the persuadee, and identify the breathing pattern.

Pace the Person's Voice

Some top salespeople have attended acting school to learn different accents in order to sound like others without mimicking them. Your voice is a very powerful tool for reflecting the persuadee's mannerisms. "Voice quality" is a mysterious thing. It involves pitch, nasality, volume, breathiness, harshness, and timbre. "Timbre" is the quality that tells you the instrument you hear being played is a violin, not a flute or a piano.[21] You are capable of adjusting your voice to sound like almost any other human being.

As you reflect the conscious and unconscious mannerisms of the persuadee, you will notice that he or she likes to be with you and wants to communicate with you. A trusting bond has been established. Now is your chance to prove your trustworthiness by making *suggestions* that would be appropriate for the persuadee. Base the suggestions on your knowledge of the speaker, and your background, experience, values, and feelings. You are treating the persuadee as a client, instead of a statistic.

Suggesting

If your only purpose of communication is to gain rapport, your communication may only include identifying and reflecting. But if you are interested in sharing something of yourself, knowledge of your product, or an idea for your mutual benefit, *suggestions* are appropriate. Milton Erickson called suggestions at this stage of persuasive listening, "leading." Leading is helping the client bridge from where he or she is to where you are. You can call someone over to where you are, you can drag them there, or you can meet them where they are and lead them back. But, nobody wants to be controlled. People want to make their own decisions, even if their conclusion is wrong and yours is right. They want and deserve the freedom to choose.

People tend to hire individuals that are like themselves. We tend to marry people that are similar to us. We like people who are like us, and find it difficult to disagree with people that we like. Consequently, the better we are at pacing, the more influence we have. If we truly reflect the mannerisms, thoughts, and feelings of the speaker, we reflect his or her inner life and will naturally begin to empathize with him or her. The end result is that, intuitively, we will know when to make verbal suggestions. It is morally imperative that we are true to that empathy and that we are as transparent to the persuadee as he or she has been to us. Our suggestions need to be coherent with our understanding of what the persuadee needs and wants.

Anthony Allesandra compared traditional sales methods with nonmanipulative sales methods (See Table 8.1).

Understanding and meeting people's needs was what Paul, the apostle, had in mind when he said, "I have become all things to all men in order that I might win some."

Before making your suggestions, see if you have rapport. If you make a move and your persuadee follows with a similar

TRADITIONAL SELLING	VERSUS	NONMANIPULATIVE SELLING
Salesperson oriented		Client oriented
Creates needs		Discovers needs
"Talks at" client		"Discusses with" client
Makes sales		Makes customers
Inflexible		Adaptable
Increases fear and distrust		Increases trust and understanding.[22]

Table 8.1. Contrast in selling styles

movement, you are in the enviable, yet responsible, position of making a suggestion that has a high probability of being accepted, all other things being equal. Meet the person in his or her "space" and build a mutual trust as you begin understanding him or her. Eventually, that person will want to understand you better and will enter your "space" to receive what you have to share. "Overeager salespeople move too quickly into their presentation. . . . Like overeager batters, they swing at every ball that comes their way. They encounter stalls and objections because they have not taken the time or applied the skill to build respect and trust."[23]

The effective listener can learn the art and skill of "communisuasion," and will have the privilege and responsibility of powerful influence over those with whom he or she communicates. The influence will grow as long as the listener is faithful to this skill and makes suggestions that are congruent with the values of life.

If people are not responsive to your suggestions, if your ideas do not have the influence they deserve, if you are not a persuasive listener, you should listen to the words of Dostoyevski, in *The Brothers Karamazov.* "If people around you are spiteful, callous, and will not hear you, fall down before them and beg for their forgiveness; for in truth you are to blame for their not wanting to hear you."

N I N E

Profit from the Interpretation of Nonverbal Communication

As a man thinks in his heart, so is he.
—Hebrew proverb

Learning is acquired by reading books, but the much more necessary learning, the knowledge of the world, can only be acquired by reading men, and studying all the various editions of them.—
Lord Chesterfield, "Letters to His Son"

U p to 90 percent of what a person communicates is transmitted nonverbally through posture, facial expressions, gestures, tone of voice, and many other factors. Subconsciously you understand nonverbal communication and respond to it with nonverbal communication of your own. When the boss says, "nice job," but his voice is less than enthusiastic, you rightly conclude that it wasn't a nice job. The slope of your shoulders and the bend in your neck communicate that you understand. When a white, middle-class American is unable to look at you at least 30 to 60 percent of the time during your conversation, you conclude that he or she is uninterested and excuse yourself. Many of the interpretations of nonverbal communication lie in the subconscious. To completely understand a message, you must attend to the speaker's nonverbal as well as verbal communication.

LISTENING WITH THE WHOLE BODY

You cannot *not* communicate. When you are listening to the speaker, fully concentrating on what he or she is saying, your body is speaking. Your responsive body language provides the speaker with almost constant feedback. The speaker can tell if you are listening and how much you are listening. When you are most attentive, your body moves in time and intensity with the speaker's voice.[1]

Six students were trained in "attending behavior," or the ability to concentrate on the speaker, by psychologists Allen Ivey and Eugene Oetting. During this experiment, the students attended a class to observe the effect of their nonverbal communication on the lecturer. The students began with non-attending behavior, and the professor, unaware of their plan, methodically read his notes without gestures. At a predetermined signal, the students began demonstrating interest and the professor perked up. Within thirty seconds he gave his first gesture, his pace quickened, and the class took on new life. The class changed as a result of student interest. Eventually, the students stopped listening. The teacher, after an awkward attempt to engage the students, resumed the deliberate lecture with which he started the class.[2] This experiment in "whole body listening" demonstrates the potential power of the listener.

In order to influence the speaker in a positive way or even fully understand him or her, the listener must carefully attend to the speaker's nonverbal cues. All nonverbal communication must be interpreted within context. Communication does not take place in a vacuum. As the context changes, the interpretation may also change. On one occasion, the client's legs were crossed and his toes were pointing directly at the salesman. The salesman interpreted this as positive interest. On another occasion, the client's toes were pointing away and the salesman interpreted his posture as lack of interest. The salesman didn't know that the man in the second scene had an injured foot and had to keep it immobile. This explains why the client's toe was pointed in a direction which happened to be away from the salesman. Nonverbal communication must be interpreted in clusters. No single nonverbal cue stands alone. Crossed arms may be a sign of defensiveness or closed-mindedness. But, if this signal is not backed up by a facial expression that shows rejection, you cannot be sure of its meaning.

You learn nonverbal communication by observing it in real life, not by reading a book. The model is the strongest teacher in the world. In the presence of nonverbal communication, an effective listener's whole body automatically models the speaker. Response is more than visual.

You can learn the meaning of nonverbal communication by reflecting the nonverbal communication of others. Imitate the mode you observe, and then ask yourself how you feel and what it means. Television actors and commentators can be your models. Watch television with the volume turned down, and note the person's posture, gestures, and facial expression, and then imitate them. If your body reflects that of the television personality, and the person on the screen is depicting a character from your culture, your body will teach you what is being said. You will learn the meaning of a particular set of nonverbal cues. If you have a video cassette recorder, tape several segments of characters you can model. After you have viewed the segments and have practiced reflecting the nonverbal cues, turn up the volume. Ask yourself if the verbal communication synchronizes with the nonverbal communication. Practice using the same tone, speed, and pitch of the voice. What meaning do these qualities add to what the speaker is trying to convey? By increasing your vocabulary of nonverbal cues, you will increase your awareness. Reinforce what you learn by writing it down.

After you have practiced with television personalities, you can begin to consciously model the nonverbal cues of people in your environment. As you observe them, ask yourself what they are thinking and feeling. It may take many months, maybe even years, to consciously understand the nonverbal cues in your environment, but the payoff is worth the time and effort.

When verbal and nonverbal communication contradict each other, you should believe the latter. "Actions speak louder than words." Remember when you were afraid and didn't want to show it. Although you attempted to calm your voice, your lip was trembling and you were shivering. Your body's actions gave you away.

What is true of nonverbal communication in your culture may not be true in another culture. Facial expressions are universal, but gestures are not. Burping after a good meal is a sign of satisfaction and gratitude in the Mongolian culture, but it is a sign of crudeness and bad manners in the United States. Standing within a foot of a business associate may be required in Brazil to reinforce interest, but it is intrusive in the United States.

The more attentive you are and the more you consciously try to mirror the speaker's body language, the more likely your entire body will synchronize with the speaker, helping you to understand what the speaker is trying to communicate. Recently developed high-speed cameras can pick up what the naked eye cannot see. An attentive listener unconsciously mimics the physical movements of the speaker within 50 milliseconds. An effective speaker is like an orchestra conductor leading the movement of his audience.[3]

CATALOG OF NONVERBAL CUES

The following pages contain a catalog of nonverbal cues. Review the catalog to increase your awareness of what to listen to. The catalog provides suggestions to get you started in your observations. The list is not exhaustive because the number of cues and combinations of cues is almost infinite. Furthermore, one cue does not necessarily provide enough information for an accurate interpretation.

Review the nonverbal categories. To reinforce your learning, refer back to the list and record your observations while viewing one or more television characters from your culture. You have been assimilating your culture's nonverbal cues all of your life, and subconsciously you know what they mean. "What you learn from is the feedback you get from your own body as you try to match the body language being demonstrated. . . . No set of detailed written instructions will replace the feedback you get from your body. . . ."[4] writes Dr. Elgin. These exercises will help you become aware of the information that is buried in the past. So, while you reflect nonverbal cues, ask your body what it is saying. Keep the catalog in front of you while practicing with the television. This will help you be more aware of and better able to interpret the cues sent by the five people with whom you are trying to improve communication.

Remember the two cardinal rules: (1) All cues need to be interpreted in context and in clusters. No single cue is sufficient to determine its own meaning. No cue can be correctly interpreted out of context. (2) If you accurately model the nonverbal cues from your native culture and ask yourself what they mean, you will gain a conscious understanding of them.

Cues Using Time

In my early years of conducting workshops, I wasn't as aware of nonverbal communication as I am now. If midway through the morning I saw someone glance at his watch, it usually didn't bother me. Even if he took a moment to stare at his watch, I wasn't bothered. I didn't realize it was time for a coffee break until he took off his watch and shook it![5]

TIME CUES TO OBSERVE

1. Promptness or delay in recognizing the presence of another, or in responding to his communication.
2. A glance at a clock, or ignoring any reference to time.
3. Amount of time one is willing to spend communicating with a person. Note relative amounts of time spent on various topics.
4. Preference for or aversion to a time of day, week, or month.

Turn on the television and observe a character with the volume turned down. Is any reference to time evident in his or her nonverbal cues? Note the cluster of accompanying nonverbal cues. If you recognize what you think are relevant nonverbal cues related to time, mirror the behavior and ask yourself what it means.

Description of observation _____

Cluster of supporting cues _____

Meaning of nonverbal cue(s) _____

Cues Using Gestures

All human beings gesture while they talk. In some people, the movement is so slight, it goes unnoticed. In others, gestures are emphatic and can be misinterpreted.

Jerry Wendslow was the town pharmacist. Everyday he walked between his home and the drugstore. He saved a lot of time by taking a shortcut through the local cemetery. One night in early autumn, after filling a record number of prescriptions, Jerry finally headed home. Clouds obscured the moon and fog blanketed the ground. He never noticed the grave that had been dug that afternoon. Jerry fell in.

He tried to climb out, but the grave was deep and the ground was soft. His efforts were futile. He cried out, but nobody heard him. After thirty minutes, he gave up and decided to wait for the burial party to arrive the next morning. Curling up in the corner of the grave, he fell sound asleep.

Two hours later Jeb Plowman passed by the cemetery with his dog Blue. They were hunting the raccoon that had been eating the corn on Jeb's nearby farm. Suddenly, Blue spotted the culprit and chased him into the graveyard. Jeb was very superstitious and the last place he wanted to be at midnight was in a graveyard. But, he had been hunting the raccoon for a long time. By the sound of his barks, Blue had treed that 'coon.

Jeb steeled his jaw, set his nerves, and ran after his barking hound. He bumped into six tombstones before falling into the same grave that had swallowed Jerry two hours earlier. Jeb threw down his rifle and, in a panic, began to scream and claw at the sides of the grave.

After fifteen minutes of frenetic effort, he paused to take a deep breath before commencing action. But, his screams had awakened Jerry. Knowing that Jeb's efforts were futile, Jerry suddenly reached out in the pitch darkness, put his hand on Jeb's shoulder, and advised solemnly, "Give it up, you'll never get out." The next thing you know, Jeb was gone.

On occasion, a misunderstood hand gesture can be helpful. But don't count on it!

HAND AND ARM GESTURES TO OBSERVE

1. Symbolic hand and arm gestures like "that was close," "stop," or "come on."
2. Literal hand and arm gestures that indicate size or shape like "it was this big" or "it was square, like this."
3. Demonstrations of how something happened or how to do something. For example, "To be effective in your presentation to the marketing group, stand on this side of the flip chart, face the group, and point with your left hand."

Again, observe your character on television with the volume turned down. Note his or her gestures and accompanying nonverbal cues. Model the behavior and ask yourself what it means.

Description of observation _____

Cluster of supporting cues _____

Meaning of nonverbal cue(s) _____

SIGNALS OR COMMANDS TO OBSERVE

1. Snapping fingers
2. Holding finger to lips
3. Pointing
4. Staring directly at a person
5. Shrugging shoulders
6. Waving
7. Nodding head
8. Winking
9. Shaking head

Once again, observe your television character(s) with the volume turned down. Are any of the above cues evident? If so, model the behavior and ask yourself what it means.
Description of observation _____
Cluster of supporting cues _____
Meaning of nonverbal cue(s) _____

TOUCHING CUES TO OBSERVE

1. Tapping on shoulder
2. Caressing
3. Poking another with finger
4. Slapping on back
5. Patting on top of head
6. Handshake

Is your television character using any of the touching cues? If so, model the behavior and ask yourself what it means.
Description of observation _____
Cluster of supporting cues _____
Meaning of nonverbal cue(s) _____

Cues Using Body Posture

A soldier on Guadalcanal described his "deadly combat" with his mortal enemy.

"The foxhole I found was so small I had to drop into it sideways," he said. "I awoke when I felt a hand on my chest. I swung at the guy and we rolled out of the hole. I felt him groping at my side as I stood to loosen my machete, but he wasn't making a sound. I couldn't get at my weapon and he hit me on the hip. But there wasn't any strength behind the blow. When I felt a thousand needles penetrating my right hand, I realized what had happened—I had been attacked by my own right arm, which had fallen asleep when I lay on top of it."[6]

Asking your body what nonverbal communication means is only helpful if your body is functioning properly.

BODY POSTURE CUES TO OBSERVE

1. Leaning forward
2. Slouching
3. Arms crossed in front
4. Arms crossed in back
5. Crossing legs
6. Seated facing other person
7. Head looking down at floor

Turn the volume down on your television and try to identify some body posture cues. The list above represents only a few cues. Model the posture and ask yourself what your body means in that position.

Description of observation _____

Cluster of supporting cues _____

Meaning of nonverbal cue(s) _____

Cues Using Body Distance

A listening workshop was presented to personnel directors of multinational corporations from several different countries. I asked the director from Brazil if four feet would be an appropriate distance for face-to-face business communication in his country. He excitedly replied, "Oh, no, that's too far away. We like to get close, like this." He leaned toward the man sitting next to him so that he was about a foot away. Then, I asked the man sitting next to the Brazilian director how close he preferred to be while conducting business. He was from Germany, and he brought the house down when he pointed to the Brazilian and said, "about six feet from *him*!" Remember, your body only knows the nonverbal communication practiced in your culture. So, focus on television characters from your culture.

BODY DISTANCE CUES TO OBSERVE

1. Moves away when other moves toward
2. Moves toward when other moves away
3. Takes initiative in moving away or toward
4. Distance widens or narrows gradually

Turn the volume down on your television and notice the distance between your character and other persons in the scene. Model the position in your mind and imagine your body in a similar situation. Position yourself in a similar manner and ask yourself what it means.

Description of observation _____

Cluster of supporting cues _____

Meaning of nonverbal cue(s) _____

Cues Using Voice Quality

Voice quality is an underrated element in the interpretation of nonverbal communication. Quality refers to the way a voice sounds based on characteristics such as pitch, volume, and degree of nasality. The impact of voice qualities on listeners was graphically demonstrated by a research project on nonverbal communication conducted by Peter Blanck and associates. One of the findings concerned trials in which the judge knew the defendant had a previous record of felonies. By law, the jury is not privy to this information unless the defendant takes the stand. The juries in these cases said they were unaware of any biases on the part of the judges. Yet, their verdicts were twice as likely to be "guilty" than in cases in which the charges were as serious, but defendants had no record of felonies. "When videotapes were analyzed by independent raters, they found that the judges' tone of voice, rather than anything in their words or body movements, communicated the strongest, most negative messages."[7] Turn on your television set, and observe your character with the volume turned up. Listen for the following voice qualities.

VOICE QUALITY CUES TO OBSERVE

1. Tone of voice

    a. Flat, monotone, absence of feeling
    b. Bright, vivid changes of inflection
    c. Strong, confident, firm
    d. Weak, hesitant, shaky

2. Rate of speech

    a. Fast
    b. Medium
    c. Slow

3. Volume of voice

    a. Loud
    b. Medium
    c. Soft

4. Diction

    a. Precise versus careless
    b. Regional (colloquial) differences
    c. Consistency of diction

5. Pitch

    a. High

    b. Low

    c. Changes in pitch

Use your voice to mimic the qualities you heard and ask yourself what they mean.

Description of observation _____

Cluster of supporting cues _____

Meaning of verbal cue(s) _____

Cues Using Facial Expressions

The face is the primary site for the display of feelings and nonverbal effects. In *Unmasking the Face, A Guide to Recognizing Emotions from Facial Expressions,* Paul Ekman and William V. Friesen provide research that supports and expands on the observations of Charles Darwin. Darwin believed that facial expressions were transcultural. Ekman and Friesen confirmed this and analyzed how every muscle in the face works, relative to six transcultural facial expressions. Their results provide "facial blueprints which will improve your ability to spot emotion in others, and help you to be aware of what your facial muscles are saying about your feelings."[8] We know that each of these facial expressions has the same meaning in Canada and in Japan. Some researchers think that facial expressions are subject to involuntary responses.

Six basic facial expressions and their various combinations are revealed in three major facial areas. The six expressions are: surprise, fear, disgust, anger, happiness, and sadness. These expressions may appear in combinations. For example, surprise and fear or happiness and surprise may be simultaneous. They may also appear so quickly that you have to be looking for these facial expressions or you'll miss them.

The three major facial areas are the brow, the eyes, and the lower face. To get an accurate reading of the facial expression, you need to observe the characteristics of the three facial areas. Practice observing the facial expressions of television characters. This exercise will make it easier and more helpful for you to recognize the feelings displayed in photographs. You can also recognize your feelings by observing your own facial expressions. Your feelings can be responsible for awesome success or terrible failure. Yet as Ekman and Friesen say, "We know less about our feelings than we do about our teeth, our car, or our neighbor's escapades."[9]

You will benefit by practicing the facial expressions with a mirror. When you make the facial expressions, your body will know what they mean. The catalog of cues will help you focus your attention on the muscles that reveal surprise, fear, disgust, anger, happiness, or sadness. Because of the explicit research conducted by Ekman and Friesen, we know and can share with you what each means. At the end of the catalog of facial cues you'll find an enjoyable exercise that will test your ability to recognize combinations of expressions.

BROW CUES TO OBSERVE

1. Raised, so that they are curved, and high show surprise
2. Raised and drawn together show fear
3. Lowered brow or lowering the upper eyelid shows disgust
4. Skin below the brow, triangulated with inner corner up, shows sadness

Using a mirror, move your brow as described in the list above, then observe a television character's brow. Model the character's brow and ask yourself what it means.
Description of observation _____

Cluster of supporting cues _____

Meaning of nonverbal cue(s) _____

EYE CUES TO OBSERVE

1. Sparkling
2. Teary
3. Wide-eyed
4. Eye contact

    a. Looking at a specific object
    b. Looking down
    c. Looking steadily at a person
    d. Staring or glaring
    e. Looking at others, but turning away when looked at
    f. Covering eyes with hands
    g. Frequency of looking at another

5. Position of eyelids

    a. Are the eyelids wide open?
    b. Is the upper lid raised and the lower lid drawn, so that the white of the eye (the sclera) is visible both above and below the iris? If so, the eyes are displaying surprise.
    c. Is the upper eyelid raised, exposing sclera, and the lower eyelid tense and drawn up? If so, the eyes are displaying fear.
    d. If lines are visible below the lower lid, and the lid is pushed up but it is not tense, the eyes are showing disgust.
    e. If the upper lid is tense and lowered by the brow, the face *might* be showing anger. Likewise, if the eyes have

a hard stare and a bulging appearance, the eyes are *probably* displaying anger. (The entire cluster of non-verbal cues must be in place before you can ascertain that the expression is anger.)[10]

f. If wrinkles are visible below the lower eyelid (it may be raised, but not tense), the eyes are displaying happiness. If crowsfeet wrinkles go outward from the outer corners of the eyes, this is an additional sign of happiness.

g. If the inner corner of the upper eyelid is raised, the eyes are displaying sadness.

Use a mirror to observe your various eyelid positions and affirm their meaning. Observe a television character's eyelid positions and try to identify the meaning being conveyed.

Description of observation _____

Cluster of supporting cues _____

Meaning of nonverbal cue(s) _____

LOWER FACE CUES TO OBSERVE The lower face includes the nose, cheeks, and lips. The distinct position of the lips is the most apparent cue in the lower face.

1. If the lower jaw drops open and the teeth part, but the mouth is not tense or stretched, the person is probably surprised.

2. When the mouth is open and the lips are either tensed lightly and drawn back or stretched and drawn back, fear is evident.

3. If the nose is wrinkled, disgust is *probably* evident.

4. Raised cheeks are another sign of disgust.

5. When the lips are pressed firmly together with the corners drawn down, the person *may* be angry.

6. If the lips are open and tensed in a squarish shape as if shouting, anger is *probably* being displayed. (Unless signs of anger are visible in all three areas of the face, the interpretation is uncertain.)
7. If the corners of the lips are drawn back and up, the person is happy.
8. When a wrinkle (the nasolabial fold) runs down from the nose to the outer edge beyond the lip corners, happiness is evident.
9. When the corners of the lips are down and/or the lips are trembling, the person is sad.

Use a mirror to practice identifying and affirming the various positions of the lips, nose, and cheeks. Then, turn down the volume on the television and observe a character's lower face. Are any of the above cues evident? If so, model them and ask yourself what they mean.

Description of observation _____

Cluster of supporting cues _____

Meaning of nonverbal cue(s) _____

Now, turn up the volume to see if the facial expressions match the words and voice qualities.

SKIN CUES TO OBSERVE Admittedly, skin is difficult to observe on television, but you may be able to pick up some of the following cues. By observing these cues, you will be more conscious of their presence with associates.

1. Pallor
2. Perspiration
3. Blushing
4. Goose bumps

Try to notice these cues on your television character(s). It may be easier to concentrate on skin cues if the volume is turned down. If any skin cues are evident, imagine yourself in a similar situation and ask yourself what it would mean.

Description of observation _____

Cluster of supporting cues _____

Meaning of nonverbal cue(s) _____

You have gained insight and sensitivity to nonverbal communication by reading through the catalog of cues. By completing some of the exercises, you will gain insight and unforgettable experience. You will make great strides in understanding the "Language of Listening" by repeating each exercise until you are certain of what you are observing, hearing, and feeling. You can spend a few minutes at a time or a few hours at a time. Whatever your schedule, you will profit; and you can always pick up where you left off.

FACE RECOGNITION EXERCISE # 1

The facial drawings in the following exercises were prepared by humorist Roger Petersen who also wrote the accompanying scenario. The faces below depict five of the six basic transcultural facial expressions identified by Ekman and Friesen (*happiness, sadness, fear, anger, surprise, or disgust*). As you read the story, "A Business Trip with the Boss," choose the word that fits the facial expression. Check your answers at the end of the scenario.

A Business Trip with the Boss

You are flying to Denver with your boss for a two-day meeting with an important client. You are supposed to meet your boss at the airport ticket counter. You arrive before he does and wait patiently. Ten minutes later you see your boss come down the escalator. As he approaches you, you compliment him on his new suit.

Figure 9.1. Facial expression #1.

When you arrive at check-in, the attendant tells your boss there is no record of a reservation for him.

Figure 9.2. Facial expression #2.

The attendant keeps searching and eventually locates your boss's reservation, for a party of two, under your name. You board the plane and take off. You both start flipping through the airline's flight magazine, and your boss becomes engrossed in a photo essay on hunger conditions in India and Ethiopia.

Figure 9.3. Facial expression #3.

Thirty minutes later lunch is served. You ask your boss how he likes the Salisbury steak.

Figure 9.4. Facial expression #4.

The pilot announces that you should be landing in Denver in about forty minutes. Suddenly the airplane takes an abrupt and rapid nose dive.

Figure 9.5.   Facial expression #5.

A few seconds later the plane levels off and slowly gains altitude. The pilot apologizes for the unexpected air turbulence and assures a smooth ride for the duration of the trip.

How did you do? Answers: A. Happiness, B. Anger, C. Sadness, D. Disgust, and E. Fear.

FACE RECOGNITION EXERCISE #2

The next exercise is a little tougher. The subtleties of facial expressions are numerous. Changes in the forehead, eyebrows, and eyelids may reflect one emotion; while the cheeks, nose, lips, and chin may reveal a different emotion. The two emotions blend into one facial expression to show sad-angry expressions, angry-afraid expressions, surprise-fearful expressions, happy-surprise expressions, and numerous others. Even within the same emotion there are numerous variations. For example, surprise is an emotion with many variations. There is a questioning surprise, a dumbfounded surprise, a dazed surprise, and other subtleties.

Figure 9.6.   Facial expression #6—mixture of emotions.

Cover the lower part of the first face with your hand and interpret the expression in the upper part of the face. Then cover the upper part of the face to interpret the expression in the lower part of the face. Emotions depicted in faces frequently express a combination of feelings so rapidly that they are often missed. Very quick "microexpressions" can reveal emotions the person is attempting to conceal.[11] We often even miss the "macroexpressions" that last two or three seconds because we are not looking at the other person.

Observe the mouth. Notice the corners of the lips drawn back and up, and a wrinkle (the nasolabial fold) running down from the nose to the outer edge beyond each lip corner. When either of these are evident, the person is usually happy. These characteristics in the lower part of the face, the mouth, depict happiness.

Observe the upper face. The brows are raised and drawn together. The wrinkles in the forehead are in the center, not

across the entire forehead. The upper eyelid is raised, exposing sclera, and the lower eyelid is tense and drawn up. These
characteristics in the upper face depict fear.

The combination of expressions on the first face is typical
of a person trying to conceal fear, or who is both happy and
scared. For example, a parent tells a friend that his or her
teenage son just got his driver's license. The parent may have
mixed emotions, feeling both pride and apprehension.

Figure 9.7.   Facial expression #7—mixture of emotions.

Now, look at the second face and try to recognize the
combination of emotions. Cover the lower part of the face and
observe the characteristics in the upper face. The brows are
raised so that they are curved and high. The skin below the
brow is stretched and wrinkles go across the forehead. The
upper eyelids are drawn down so that the white of the eye, the
sclera, shows above and below the iris. These are characteristics of surprise.

Now cover the upper part of the face and observe the
characteristics of the lower face. The mouth is similar to the

mouth in the first face, and the corners of the lips are drawn back and up. The only difference in the second figure is that the mouth is open, exposing the teeth. These are characteristics of happiness. This type of facial blend occurs when someone is surprised by something pleasant, such as an unexpected birthday party.

Cues Using Physical Settings

> *Space management may well be the most
> ignored and powerful tool for inducing culture
> change and speeding up innovation projects and
> task execution in general.—Tom Peters*

The study of space and a person's relationship to space has been the subject of scientific investigation. Large numbers of people confined to small areas of space, without appropriate safeguards, produce antisocial behavior. It is not a coincidence that people in large cities, surrounded by crowds, are less likely to engage in casual conversation with a stranger. They insulate themselves to protect their privacy. Small-town residents do not share this inhibition because their greater physical space provides them with privacy; therefore, they prefer to be more open.

The physical environment will either enhance or hinder effective communication. Which of the three office arrangements will be most conducive to effective communication and why? (See Figure 9.8.)

In diagram A the desk is a barrier and the two visitor chairs are pushed back against the wall. The large space behind the desk chair communicates power, dominance, and control. In diagram B the barriers are modified. Diagram C provides the best setting for effective communication. Physical barriers are removed and the space is equally divided.

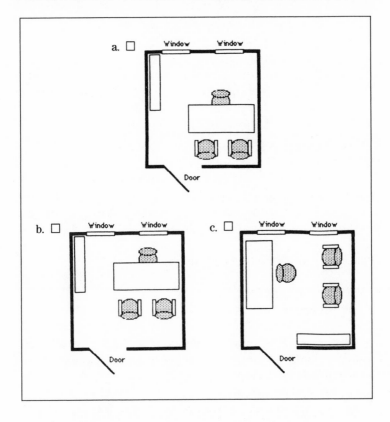

Figure 9.8. Three possible office settings.

OFFICE SETTING CUES TO OBSERVE

1. Neat, ordered, organized
2. Untidy, haphazard, careless
3. Casual versus formal
4. Warm versus cold colors
5. Soft versus hard materials
6. Slick versus varied textures

7. Cheerful and lively versus dull and drab
8. "Discriminating" taste versus tawdry
9. Expensive or luxurious versus shabby or Spartan

Turn on your television and focus on the setting of a room. Note the arrangement of the physical setting and ask yourself what feelings the elements in the room generate.

Description of the setting _____

Feelings the setting conveys _____

A more personal element to notice in the physical setting is the person's clothing and what it conveys. You can increase your awareness of this subject by reading *Dress for Success*. We suggest only two general categories relating to dress.

PERSONAL DRESS CUES TO OBSERVE

1. Bold versus unobtrusive
2. Stylish versus nondescript

Observe your television characters and ask yourself what cues you would be sending if you were similarly dressed.

Description of the clothing _____

Feelings the clothing conveys _____

In our final cluster of "setting cues," observe the person's physical position in relation to the setting and others in the scene. The following list will encourage your thinking.

PHYSICAL POSITION CUES TO OBSERVE

1. Physical objects between speaker and others

    a. Desk
    b. Chair
    c. Table
    d. Other

2. Speaker seated or standing or moving
3. Speaker in center of room
4. Speaker in back of room
5. Speaker toward front of room
6. Speaker in front of door or exit
7. Speaker seated while other(s) stand(s)
8. Speaker standing while other(s) sit(s)
9. Speaker moves toward or away from listener
10. Listener moves toward or away from speaker

Observe your television character and ask yourself what his or her position conveys. How would you feel if you were in a similar position? Imagine yourself as the character and write down what you think you would feel. Imagine yourself as someone else in that room observing the television personality. What would the person be conveying to you?

Description of the physical position _____

Feeling the physical position conveys _____

ATTITUDE SENSING CUES TO OBSERVE Attitude is primarily revealed by nonverbal cues. A person's attitude, unlike a feeling, exists for a longer time. Consequently, one's *attitude* will determine his or her destiny. Most top executives concur that a positive attitude plays a significant role in their success. An aware, decisive, and committed person will expect and deal with major problems. An attitude of frustration, defiance, or resignation is a hindrance in dealing with even minor problems. Knowing an associate's attitude toward an issue or person will help you be successful in the relationship.

The "Osgood Attitude Curve," developed by Dr. Donald Osgood after thirty years as an internal consultant for IBM, depicts the path our feelings frequently take when we are confronted with a new situation in either our personal or professional life. Finding one's position on this curve and learning how to move to a positive position has saved thousands of careers. (See Figure 9.9.)

We usually begin a new job or personal relationship *idealistically,* superficially happy, and enthusiastically. Before long we realize that there is a gap between the real situation and what we expected. We become *frustrated,* irritated, exasperated, worried, anxious, chagrined, disappointed, and dissatisfied.

If we do not handle the situation productively, we become *defiant,* angry, disobedient, insubordinate, rebellious, affronting, and confrontational. We try to make the organization or relation fit our expectations. This approach encourages a negative reaction on the attitude curve.

This downward plunge causes us to lose momentum and become *resigned,* apathetic, uninvolved, passive, submissive, and accepting. This is when the "divorce" takes place in the heart and mind of a married couple, even if a legal divorce is not sought. This is when the professional has "died on the job," but is still there physically and is counted on the payroll.

If you are familiar with the language of effective listening, you can help yourself and others become *aware* of what is happening. When you are aware of the problem, you can recognize your need to change and accept the responsibility to change. Osgood says, "Often an individual can be brought to awareness by a statement of the real situation. For instance, a supervisor might say to an employee, 'Ann, I'm worried about you. I feel that you are drifting, and I'm afraid of what this may lead to in a few months.' Here's another example that deals with personal feelings at home: 'Harry, I have the feeling that the children and I aren't as important to you as we once were.' This constructive, straightforward statement of the situation can lead to a helpful discussion, if the person starting the discussion couples it with real concern for the person."[12]

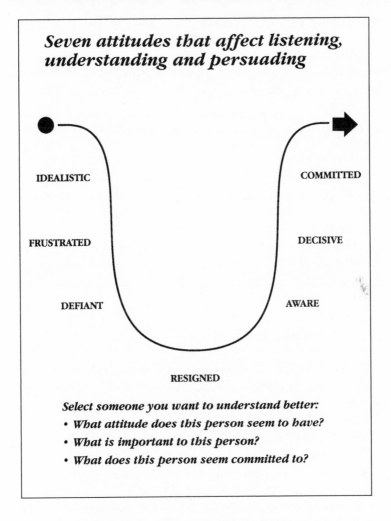

Figure 9.9. The Osgood Attitude Curve.

Awareness usually leads to *decisiveness*. Making the decision is the first step. You become active, resolute, and positive. From positive awareness will flow *enlightened commitment*.

We don't expect perfection and we have learned how to live with some ambiguities, but we strive for excellence. Now we become involved, motivated, coherent, and happy.

If you are familiar with a person's attitude, you can meet his or her attitude and stay in "sync," or lead him or her to a more positive attitude. When reading attitudes, it is important to read all of the sensed nonverbal cues, including facial and vocal expressions, gestures, postures, time cues, and setting cues.

Turn the volume up on your television, choose a character, and practice identifying the seven attitudes.

1. Idealistic
2. Frustrated
3. Defiant
4. Resigned
5. Aware
6. Decisive
7. Enlightened Commitment

Imagine yourself as the character, reflect his or her non-verbal communication, and ask yourself which of the seven attitudes you would have if you were communicating like him or her.

Description of attitude(s) _____

Feelings the attitude(s) convey(s) _____

You have been observing nonverbal communication all of your life. As an infant, you babbled the seventy sounds that make up the sound system of all human language.[13] From the day you were born, your body synchronized with the nonverbal communication surrounding you. You were capable of synchronizing with and learning any of the world's languages. As you got older, you discriminated between sounds, concentrating only on those that were used by your parents and others in your environment. Your body continued to synchronize with the physical movements of the speakers around you and your entire body learned the language. Over the years you have added to your knowledge, so that, subconsciously, you are an expert in both body language and other nonverbal communication of your culture.

Now, by consciously observing another person's body language, your understanding of his or her communication increases up to 90 percent. A true "meeting of meanings" will come with your growing understanding of people. This greater understanding will release the potential of your relationship. You can't learn nonverbal communication reading a book. The only way to learn is to practice reading people— "all the various editions of them." Enjoy the adventure!

T E N

Improve Listening Through Effective Notetaking

*Evidence points out that trained notetakers are
better listeners—Dr. Ralph Nichols*

Notetaking is an important part of our culture. I keep a pad and a pencil next to the telephone, so I'm ready to take notes when the telephone rings. Usually the first fifteen seconds of a conversation give the critical information which includes the name of the caller and the purpose of the call.[1] Conference tables prepared for business sessions are supplied with yellow, lined legal pads. Associates enter a manager's office equipped with a pen and paper, ready to take notes. Students diligently take notes in class, and write notes to other students!

Dr. Nichols describes the frustration that many notetakers experience. "The notetaker is thoroughly determined to record what he hears. The speaker starts talking and the man with the yellow pad assumes the writing position. As the words strike his ears, he commences to write. From long experience, he knows that notetaking is a tense race, pitting his penmanship agility against the talker's rate of speech. Soon the man who is talking is winning the race. Good handwriting is discarded in favor of something more speedy—a hasty, illegible scribble. But still it's impossible to keep up with the talk. So the notetaker now resorts to a telegraphic writing style with incomplete sentences and abbreviated words. Any chance this system might have had to work is lost by the time it is put into

Figure 10.1. Effective listeners know how and when to take notes.

use; for the notetaker has met an insolvable problem. Because he is concentrating on notetaking, he has lost track of what the talker is saying. What he is hearing doesn't even make sense anymore. The telegraphic style deteriorates to doodling, which becomes the listener's main function with the notepad, until the talk is finished."[2]

In about the fifth grade we were taught to take notes and write papers using a specific outline. We began with Roman numeral "I" for the first main point. Capital letter "A" headed the first subpoint, Arabic "1" followed the first subpoint under "A," and lower case "a" followed the first subpoint under "1," etc. This was a very precise method, but we were not informed that people do not think according to outlines. To become successful in taking notes we need to adapt our notetaking method to the style of the speaker's presentation. This is a form of synchronization.

WHY TAKE NOTES?[3]

You cannot concentrate on taking notes and on listening to what the speaker is saying at the same time. During notetaking you lose some of your attentiveness towards the speaker. In addition, desks are covered, and drawers, cabinets, notebooks, and briefcases are filled with notes that have never been read, are inadequate, inaccurate, illegible, and incomplete. If you are an effective listener, why bother to clutter your mind and desk by taking notes?

The main reason for taking notes is to remember more of what's been said. Short-term memory is less than twenty seconds, and little can be done to improve this, other than to concentrate more fully on what the speaker is saying. However, we have all the mental power necessary to remember what we need to retrieve from short-term memory. It doesn't take twenty seconds to write a skillful note.

Long-term memory, anything over twenty seconds, can be greatly enhanced by notetaking. Even if you put your notes in a drawer and throw the key away, if you are a *skilled* notetaker, you will retain more of what the speaker said. This is because skillful notetaking engages most of your senses in processing the key elements of the message.

During notetaking you experience more of the message because your muscles are involved in writing about what you see and hear. Your eyes not only see the speaker's body language but they see the words on the paper. By feeling the paper and pen, you touch what he or she communicates. The more senses involved in any learning process, the quicker and more complete the learning.

WHEN TO TAKE NOTES

Determining when to take notes is as important as how to take notes. If the message is short, only a minute or two long, and the information is not worth keeping, take notes only if it is difficult to concentrate. Disciplining yourself to take skillful notes will force you to concentrate. If you are nervous, it gives you something constructive to do. Your intense concentration demonstrates your respect for the speaker. If you can concentrate and don't need to keep the information, don't take notes.

If the message is short and the information is important, keep your notes brief or write them after the message is over. Brief notetaking means using key words. If you don't take notes during the message for fear of missing something, jot down key words as soon as the message is over. Key words give you the critical outline of the message, and you can fill in the details later.

If the information is confidential, taking notes may be inappropriate, offensive, or distracting to the speaker. In some situations it may be necessary to obtain the speaker's permission to take notes.

HOW TO TAKE NOTES

When a building or any other structure is disassembled and moved to another location to be rebuilt, knowledge of the original structure is invaluable for the reconstruction. The notetaker attempts to rebuild the thought structure of the speaker. If you discern the blueprint of the "structure," you are more likely to reconstruct the speaker's thoughts.

A college student received a big, beautiful birthday cake from home, but he had to go away for the weekend before he could cut it. He had a brief conversation with his roommate about the cake and then left. When he returned late Sunday night he was surprised to find only a small piece of cake left. "What happened to my cake?" he asked. His roommate, surprised at his concern, responded, "But just before you left you told me to take the cake." "No, I didn't," said the disappointed birthday boy, "I said 'take care.'"

Speakers have both overt and unconscious structure to their messages. The structure provides form and function to the individual's thoughts. The foundation of the speaker's message will be his or her main point or topic. Then, the speaker will build supporting points (rooms, ells, and wings) on his or her main points. The following exercise will help you build listening skills in your reconstruction projects.

IDENTIFYING OVERT ORGANIZATIONAL PATTERNS[4]

People are generally more organized than disorganized in their speech. True, in today's fast-paced society, some speakers do not take sufficient time for organization. It's very important to recognize the disorganization and make the appropriate adjustments. Listen for key words, concepts, and facts. When a

Figure 10.2. When the speaker is disorganized, effective listeners listen for facts and deduce concepts.

speaker is disorganized, the effective listener listens for facts and deduces concepts.

Once you have taken the time and made the effort to identify a speaker's organizational pattern, you will discover that he or she will tend to use the same structure all of the time.[5] People are habitual and predictable. The best way to determine what a person will do tomorrow is to look at what he or she did yesterday. Which shoe do you put on first? Which leg do you put in your pants first? Which side of your face do you shave first? The content of the message does not necessarily change when a different pattern is used, only its organization changes.

Enumeration

The first overt organizational pattern is enumeration. In this pattern, the speaker numbers his or her main thoughts. This is one of the easiest patterns to recognize and follow. Maybe that is why it is used so often in critical situations. Here's an example of the enumeration pattern.

If you are going to be all that you are capable of being, you must take control of your future by developing three skills.

1. Be willing to give 110 percent to whatever you do. As you exert more effort, you expand your ability to accomplish even more.
2. Be willing to grow, to change, to learn, and to become even more than you are now. It takes courage to change, but the benefits are worth facing the fear and conquering it.
3. Be an outstanding communicator by accepting at least 51 percent of the responsibility for all of the communication in your life. If you are the speaker, you will be 51 percent responsible for making sure the listener understands your thoughts and feelings. If you are the listener, you will be at least 51 percent responsible for making sure you understand the speaker.[6]

Enumeration is easy to spot, easy to hear, and easy to follow. When taking notes using this pattern, number the main points.

Problem and Solution

The second overt organizational pattern is problem and solution. The problem and solution pattern is often found in business situations, but it is also found in personal interactions.

Figure 10.3. Effective listeners recognize and follow the speaker's unique organizational structure.

The speaker shares a problem, its causes, and its effects, and suggests a solution or develops one or more of these components. He or she may emphasize any of the elements and de-emphasize the others. Here's an example of the problem and solution pattern.

This is the problem as I see it. We have hurdles to overcome if we are to be all that we are capable of being. In spite of the lack of commitment of our co-workers, if we are going to keep growing, we must hurdle the desire to conform and be willing to give 110 percent to the task. But that's not all, we need to get over the "comfort hurdle." We tend to grow comfortable in our circumstances and are unwilling to change. We need to be flexible, be willing to grow, and be innovative while we work toward our full potential. What can be more frustrating and difficult to hurdle than trying to listen to a co-worker who rambles, instead of getting right to the point, and who has an attention span of a millisecond when listening? If we are going to be everything that we can be, we have to take at least 51 percent of the responsibility to understand the co-worker and make sure the co-worker understands us.

The problem/solution pattern will be easy to recognize once you have tuned your ears to it. When taking notes using this pattern, divide your paper into problem(s) and solutions.

Time Sequence

The third overt organizational pattern is time sequence. The speaker puts his or her thoughts in chronological order. Typical terms used are hours, days, months, and years. He or she may start in the present and progress to the future, start in the past and progress to the future, or start in the present and regress to the past. Here's an example of the time sequence pattern.

If you are going to be everything that you can be, you must spend the first years in your job developing the habit of giving 110 percent to the task that is before you. It takes some professionals several years of trial and error to learn the importance of this commitment; others never succeed and don't understand why. After you have been in the job for five years and have established this pattern, you should be ready to change jobs, to grow, and to innovate.

The next fifteen years on the job are the most exciting and rewarding if you are willing to change with the times. After you have been around for more than fifteen years, you have a senior status, and younger co-workers want to hear what you have learned. Now you have the opportunity to multiply your productivity through the lives of others. Accepting at least 51 percent of the responsibility for all communication in your life becomes a necessity. When taking notes using this pattern, divide your comments according to the chronology of the message.

Spatial or Pictorial

The fourth overt organizational pattern is spatial or pictorial. In spatial or pictorial organization the speaker draws a picture of what he or she is trying to communicate. The secondary organizational pattern in this message is enumeration. Here's an example of the spatial or pictorial pattern.

If you are going to be everything that you are capable of being, it is necessary that you climb your personal ladder of success. "Giving 110 percent to your job" is rung number one on the ladder. The second rung is the willingness to grow, to innovate, and to change. The final rung is to be an outstanding communicator, accepting at least 51 percent of the responsibility for communication, whether you are the speaker or the listener.

Listen for word pictures and you will see this pattern. When taking notes, it will be helpful if you draw pictures. In this example you would draw a ladder and label each rung appropriately.

EXERCISE TO RECOGNIZE OVERT ORGANIZATIONAL PATTERNS
If you practice listening for these patterns you will discover that they are relatively easy to recognize. You can practice recognizing the patterns by reading the following four paragraphs and noting the primary message structure. On the space provided at the end of the paragraph put an "E" for Enumeration, a "P" for Problem or Solution, a "T" for Time Sequence, and an "S" for Spatial or Pictorial. If you recognize a primary and a secondary pattern, put the primary pattern first and the secondary one second.

1. Look, we have to realize that times have changed. Fifteen years ago if employees got out of line, they were just thrown out in the street. We could do that because we had people waiting for jobs. The trouble was that unions and management were at each other's throats, and the place was a mess. Today, we don't experience as many problems because unions and management work together better.

Now the problem is absenteeism. Who knows what will happen ten years from now? Maybe we won't be here tomorrow. But, we can't go back to the old ways. We have to find new ways to make this thing work.[7]

Primary Organizational Pattern: _____

2. Come on, you guys. You've been supervisors for ten years. The game plan hasn't changed that much. You know what to do when something happens, just like a good lineman knows what to do on the field, because he's been coached. If you play the hero, I'm going to penalize you, and if you keep it up I'm going to throw you out of the game. Don't think. React. If you have to think on a football field, you're dead. You should know what to do instinctively by now. Keep working on your job and forget about everything else.[8]

Primary Organizational Pattern: _____

3. Mary has been having trouble with the new machine. She says it runs its cycle even when she takes her hands off the buttons. Wayne says it can't happen. The machine is designed to stop when you take your hands off the buttons. Well, I'll tell you what's happening. Somebody has been putting jumpers in the machine, and I know who it is. It's the repairmen; so somebody better talk to them.

Primary Organizational Pattern: _____

4. All right, the way I see it we have three problems. First, what to do about the absenteeism in the area. Second, what to do about the guy who's stacking his work up on the floor so that he can get out early. And third, what to do about the housekeeping in the area.

Primary Organizational Pattern: _____

Answers: 1. "T" Time Sequence, 2. "S" Spatial or Pictorial, 3. "P" Problem or Solution, and 4. "E" Enumeration.

Speakers often combine these patterns, and sometimes they use different patterns than those we have illustrated. Your goal is to identify the speaker's pattern and synchronize with the speaker's structure, instead of imposing your own structure on his or her message. Take notes accordingly. Speakers will use the same pattern in about 80 percent of their messages, but if the message is too short you may miss it.

Now, think about the five people with whom you will improve your communication over the next thirty days. Can you determine what pattern or combination of patterns each person prefers? Take a moment to think about it. If you can, write what you think is their pattern(s) on the lines provided. After listening more closely to these individuals, refer back to this section and reevaluate your answers.

Initials: _____ Pattern(s) _____
Initials: _____ Pattern(s) _____
Initials: _____ Pattern(s) _____
Initials: _____ Pattern(s) _____
Initials: _____ Pattern(s) _____

IDENTIFY THE UNCONSCIOUS ORGANIZATIONAL PATTERNS

The first unconscious organizational pattern is touching or feeling. These kinesthetic speakers understand reality best through their feelings. They prefer touch and physical movement, and think or conceptualize in physical or touch terms. When you recognize this orientation in their speech, and adapt your notetaking accordingly, you will be more effective in restructuring their thoughts.

The second unconscious organizational pattern is hearing. These speakers understand concepts best through the auditory gate or through their hearing. They are called "auditory or hearing" dominant individuals because they think or conceptualize in theoretical or data-based modes. These people are characteristically critical, in the positive sense of the word. They are very effective analyzers and criticizers. They often can't understand why the person who is feeling dominant doesn't appreciate his or her conceptual organization. This inability to recognize and accept different patterns often results in "personality clashes," like those between McCoy and Spock on "Star Trek." When you hear this conceptual organization note in the speaker, play his or her tune in your notes.

The third unconscious organizational pattern is visualizing, thinking, or conceptualizing in pictures. These speakers conceptualize and understand reality best by forming pictures in their imagination. An example of this pattern is visionary Kirk of "Star Trek." When you notice this conceptual orientation in a speaker, adjust your notetaking so that you are drawing pictures on your paper.

Before reading about the fourth notetaking skill, take a few seconds to look at the triangles in Figure 10.4, and then close the book, get some paper, and write what you saw in each triangle.[9]

If you are like thousands of others who have participated in our workshops, you wrote: "Paris In The Spring," "Once In A Lifetime" and "A Bird In The Hand." Did you notice the extra "The" in the first and third triangles, and the extra "A" in the second triangle? If you did, you are unusual. Second grade students notice the extra words because they read one word at a time. Computer programmers and editors, who work with details, often notice the extra words. But readers without special training read for concepts and the main ideas. They get the concept without noticing the redundant words. Every word is not as important as every other word. When listening, pay attention to the important words, the key words. They will give you the critical concepts. A hospital superintendent showed his understanding of the concepts when he wrote

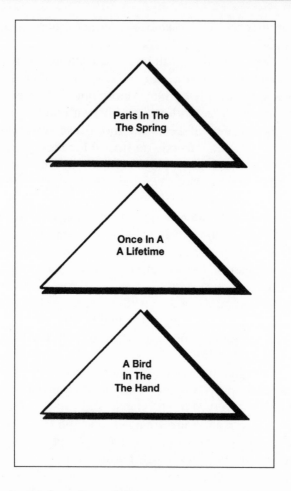

Figure 10.4. Effective listeners think or conceptualize in pictures.

"Love Blossoms" for the first triangle, "A Golden Opportunity" for the second triangle, and "A Sure Thing" for the third triangle.

The fourth unconscious organizational pattern is the skill of identifying key words. "Key words" are the words that give you the most important elements in the communication. Not all words are equally important. Read the following statement and list the four or five most important words that give the critical content. Then compare your list with mine.

This car will never sell. Its design is just plain ugly. And, look at the price, it's way too expensive for most people. You heard about the problem with maintenance; people don't like cars that break down all the time. If word gets around, this car won't sell.

Key Words _____

The key words I chose are "car," "won't sell," "design," "price," and "maintenance." If you chose those words, you are on target. In six words or less, you have enough information to capture the essence of a forty-three-word message.

Listen for the main and supporting points. The main point in the message above is that the car won't sell. The supporting points are three-fold; it's ugly, expensive, and needs maintenance. When you listen to friends and associates, listen for the key words in the conversation. It helps to feed them back to the speaker and to write them down.

INTERMITTENT NOTES

Another effective method to use with longer presentations is *Intermittent Notes*. The listener takes notes at appropriate intervals, perhaps every couple of minutes. Most speakers are organized enough to give you a clear idea of each main point as it is covered, and to provide a transition to the next point. Examples of transitional phrases are, "now I want to say" or "in addition." As you practice this notetaking skill, you will begin to easily identify transitions. "Intermittent Notes" are an abstract, a sentence, or a short summary of the main points that you heard. When the listener is finished listening, he organizes his short summaries appropriately, noting main and supporting points.

The "Intermittent Note" method enables the listener to maintain attentiveness for a maximum period of time, while still providing him with sufficient notes to reconstruct the message. If the speaker is going too fast for the listener to write entire sentences, the trained notetaker writes phrases or key words. A typical mistake that notetakers make is trying to use one method of notetaking for all situations and speakers. To be successful, you need to master the various methods and be flexible in applying them.

Even if you are not physically taking notes, it is profitable to make mental notes. Remember, you think seven to ten times faster than the speaker is talking. The average adult attention span is a few minutes. Your mind will wander unless you have learned and applied constructive methods to stay involved.

While the speaker is talking, be a detective. Prepare, sense, synchronize, interpret, evaluate, and then respond. Identify the speaker's purpose, dominant sensory mode, and preferred overt and unconscious organization pattern. Listen for key words and take notes when appropriate! You will learn more and, at the same time, raise the esteem of and build a relationship with the speaker.

E L E V E N

Conclusion

he ultimate question in this type of book—the unspoken question that lurks in the back of every reader's mind is, "Can this writer's ideas *really* change my life?"

The unequivocal answer is, "Yes, they can." This program has proven effective in the lives of thousands of managers and professionals. However, one condition exists. If you didn't apply these ideas as you read through the text, you must begin to establish a practical action plan *right now,* and then immediately put it into effect in your daily relationships. If you delay even a day or two, chances are this book will become like most others—a brief and unremarkable interlude in your otherwise busy life.

To avoid losing what you've learned, take a cue from an executive named Tom. After learning the basics of listening in a seminar, he set aside the first evening after his last class to draw up the following action plan.

- Step 1: He identified five people with whom he wanted to improve his personal communications. Two were family members: his child and his brother. Three were colleagues at work.

  These weren't the "toughest nuts," or people who had always been impossible to talk to. He would deal with the difficult ones later, after he honed his skills. Rather, the five he picked were individuals with whom he already had a decent relationship. Yet, it seemed they might draw closer to him if he could just find ways to interact on deeper levels.

- Step 2: Next, he listed specific problems he had noted in his discussions with each of these five individuals. For example, he knew that he and one of the women on his list always seemed to be "talking past" each other. Closer to home, he and his child tended to make each other angry almost every time they chatted for more than five minutes.
- Step 3: Having noted the main conversational problems, Tom began to analyze *why* each problem had developed and what he had to do to resolve it.

    Take the woman who often responded inappropriately to him. He realized that he frequently interjected his thoughts and opinions before she was finished with her point. She spoke more slowly and took longer to finish an idea than most of his other acquaintances. When he allowed her a little extra time to complete her thought sequence, their discussions became more productive.
- Step 4: He began to put his insights and observations about his five people into practice the next day. Furthermore, he continued to work regularly on his listening plan and on other conversational issues.

As Tom pursued the various objectives he had listed, he created a ripple effect. Ever-widening, concentric circles of effective communicators were now revamping the culture of his company and family. Almost imperceptibly, at first, significant changes started to take place. In fact, the major changes occurred so gradually that no one could put a finger on their starting point. Even Tom wasn't entirely sure how the process had begun, and others quickly forgot his specific role. Even though he remained an unsung hero, Tom found he reaped great personal benefits because his own circle of relationships had improved markedly. He reaped the rewards of becoming an expert in the language of effective listening.

A person committed to listening effectively to just four or five individuals can start such a program. So join the human resources movement as Tom did! Set a realistic timetable by which you expect to acquire a working knowledge of some of the skills. As Marge Blanchard says, "A goal without a timetable is just a dream." Though it may take years to become proficient in these skills, thirty days of consistent effort will produce positive results.

If you run into a brick wall, rebound and try again. Not every attempt will be successful, but if you persist you will have positive success. Success depends on your perseverance. Don't bang your head against the wall, but do give full concentration and effort to whatever you are doing at the moment. Sticking to it means doing the tough things first, and looking ahead for gratification and reward. It means yearning for progress and learning the language of effective listening. Review your material and practice with the television, then try again with your five key people. Success isn't guaranteed to the brilliant or the beautiful, only to those who are persistent.

The greatest quarterbacks complete only six out of ten passes. Top oil companies, consulting with expert geologists, find oil in only one out of ten wells. A successful television actor is turned down twenty-nine out of thirty times after auditioning for roles in commercials. Winners in the stock market make money on only two out of five investments.

As you learn from your experience, you may need to reset your goals, timetable, or action plan. Ask yourself the following questions.

1. Will the skills I want to develop have a positive impact on my overall short-term and/or long-term purposes?
2. How will these skills help my company and my family?

3. Will these skills build better communication, quality relationships, and greater personal and professional productivity?
4. Could I accept constructive criticism if I don't consistently follow through with my good intentions?
5. Should I communicate my action plan to those associates and specific family members with whom I intend to build better communication? If so, how?

If you decide to tell your associates what you are doing, don't be apologetic. Don't share too much. Do ask for their support. Ask them to let you know if you fail to accomplish what you have committed yourself to do, and to let you know when you use the Language of Effective Listening.

Through the 1990s and into the twenty-first century, managers will be hired and recognized more for their interpersonal skills than for their technical expertise. Companies that incorporate progressive human resource programs and strategies will conduct the most successful operations.

If you are interested in a live training program for your organization, an individual consultation, or a free copy of Effective Communications and Development, Inc.'s "Ten Tips to Effective Listening," fill out and mail this card, or call (914) 941-0276.

NAME _____   POSITION _____

COMPANY _____   PHONE # _____

ADDRESS _____   CITY _____

STATE _____   ZIP _____

Number of people in organization.   _____

Number of people in target training group.   _____

Time frame for workshop.   Month _____   Year _____

Potential length of program: 1-2 hour motivational session   _____
                                1, 2 or 3 day training program   _____

What did you like about the last program your people attended?   _____

_____

What did you dislike about the last program your people attended?   _____

_____

Best time to call: _____

Corporate Communication Analysis Card

Organizational Culture: A Preliminary Analysis

INSTRUCTIONS: Choose someone who you think is "typical" of your organization
and focus on him/her in answering these questions. SCORE: Almost Always = 10;
Usually = 8; Sometimes = 6; Seldom = 4; Almost Never = 2.

1. Is your organization reaching its potential for productivity?   _____
2. Do your people think your organization is tops?   _____
3. Do your people build the self esteem of customers?   _____
4. Do your people enhance and build each others' self esteem?   _____
5. Do individuals in your organization speak well of themselves?   _____
6. Do your people learn from the past, live in the present,
    but build for the future?   _____
7. When your people disagree do they remain in rapport with cus-
    tomers and/or each other?   _____
8. Do your people communicate an understanding of the thoughts
    and feelings of others before stating a contrary position?   _____
9. Can your people find a kernel of truth in a bushel of
    criticism?   _____
10. Does the job get done as requested, the first time?   _____

*   Mail this card to us and we will interpret this data for you.

© E.C.D., Inc.   P.O. Box 286, Briarcliff Manor, NY 10510   (914) 941-0276

Notes

(Complete bibliographic information found in the Bibliography.)

CHAPTER 2: ANALYZE YOUR LISTENING HABITS

1. We adapted our criteria for self-examination from the pioneer work of Dr. Ralph Nichols who was head of the Department of Rhetoric at the University of Minnesota and Dr. Lyman Steil, Dr. Nichol's successor in teaching the listening courses. Dr. Nichols and Dr. Steil collaborated in starting the International Listening Association of which Dr. Arthur Robertson is a founding member. Dr. Steil is the president of Communication Development, Inc., St. Paul, Minnesota. Dr. Steil made the Ten Bad Habits and other material quoted in this book available to Dr. Robertson in July 1980. Some of the material was subsequently published in Dr. Steil's book, *Effective Listening, Key to Your Success,* written with Dr. Larry Barker and Dr. Kitty Watson. For the Ten Bad Habits see pp. 21-29.

2. I created the "Cone of Attraction" from Dr. Steil's concept of the "Cone of Distraction."

CHAPTER 3: OVERCOME CHALLENGE NUMBER ONE WITH EFFECTIVE LISTENING

1. Rene Dubos, quoted by Schuller, *Self-Esteem: The New Reformation,* p. 18-19.

2. Dr. Bertram Brown, director of the National Institute of Mental Health, quoted by Schuller, *Self-Esteem: The New Reformation,* p. 106.

3. George Gallup, Jr., quoted by Schuller, *Self-Esteem: The New Reformation,* p. 17.

4. Samuel Schreiner, Jr., *Reader's Digest,* February 1990, pp. 140-142.

5. Blood Pressure Study, 1979, Society of Actuaries and Association of Life Insurance Medical Directors of America, quoted by Dr. Lynch, *The Language of the Heart,* p. 56.

6. Lauchland A. Henry, *The Professional Guide to Working Smarter* as quoted in *Soundview Executive Book Summaries,* July 1989, p. 4.

7. Dr. Harold Smith, "The 20% Activities That Bring 80% Payoff," *Training Today,* June 1978, p. 6.

8. Zig Ziglar, *Top Performance,* p. 129.

9. Otto Friedrich, "What Do Babies Know?" *Time,* August 15, 1983, pp. 54-55.

10. Denis Waitley, *Seeds of Greatness,* p. 110.

11. Kenneth Boa, personal conversation, 1987.

12. L. R. Wheeless, quoted by Steil, Barker, and Watson, *Effective Listening, Key to Your Success,* p. 61.

13. Steil, Barker, and Watson, Ibid., p. 2.

14. W. F. Keffe, quoted by Steil, Barker, and Watson, *Effective Listening, Key to Your Success,* p. 3.

15. Dr. Larry Barker, quoted by Steil, Barker, and Watson, *Effective Listening, Key to Your Success,* p. 5.

16. Dr. Lyman Steil, "A Longitudinal Analysis of Listening Pedagogy in Minnesota Secondary Public Schools," p. 43.

17. Denis Waitley, *Seeds of Greatness,* p. 87.

18. A concept created and used by Dr. Steil in his public workshops, "Effective Listening: Key to Your Success."

CHAPTER 4: PROFIT FROM IDENTIFYING THE SPEAKER'S PURPOSE

1. Dr. Lyman Steil shared these concepts with Dr. Robertson in July 1980 and subsequently.

2. Ibid.

3. Ibid.

4. Gary Seering and Darreshahwar Baig, *Reader's Digest,* June 1980, p. 184, quoted by Steil, Barker, and Watson in *Effective Listening, Key to Your Success,* p. 15.

CHAPTER 5: IDENTIFY AND REPAIR BREAKDOWNS IN LISTENING

1. Dr. Arthur Robertson added two components to the original model created by Dr. Lyman Steil and developed a new model which includes the concepts of preparation and

synchronization. For the original model see *Effective Listening, Key to Your Success,* Steil, Barker, and Watson, pp. 21-29.

2. Our computerized listening inventory classifies questions under the six elements of prepare, sense, synchronize, interpret, evaluate, and respond. The inventory indicates how often the participant in a training program is perceived by himself or herself, and three to five associates, to incorporate effective listening behaviors in his or her communication. The inventory responses of 145 workshop participants and 659 of their associates were statistically analyzed and have established the document as reliable.

Therefore, we are confident that changes in inventory perceptions taken a month after the workshop are due to actual perceived changes, as opposed to variations due to chance factors. Ninety-nine percent of the participants who completed our program perceived themselves as better listeners thirty to sixty days after training. Eighty-seven percent of the participants who completed our program were perceived by their associates as more effective listeners after the same length of time!

Responses from the 145 participants and their 659 associates fell into three clusters that reflect the six components of P.S.S.I.E.R.

The first and most distinct cluster contained questions in the "preparation" category. Preparation seems to be set apart from the other behaviors.

The second cluster of questions came from the synchronizing and sensing categories. Sensing and synchronizing take place so closely in time that they appear to be simultaneous. Only recently, through the use of high-speed cameras, has it been discovered that attentive listeners synchronize with the speaker within a fraction of a second of the speaker's movements. (See chapter 9.)

The third cluster of questions fit the categories defined as interpret, evaluate, and respond.

We believe it is helpful to separate and emphasize the six components described in chapter 2 so that learners can be more specific in giving their attention to problem areas. The two areas of greatest need, according to our analysis, are preparation and synchronization.

3. Bernard G. Guerney, Jr., "Relationship Enhancement: Marital/Family Therapy Training Program," April 6-9, 1990.

4. Paul de Barros, Effective Communication and Development, Inc., *Effective Listening Workshop Workbook,* 1981, p. 35.

5. de Barros, Ibid, p. 36.

6. David Augsburger, *Caring Enough to Hear and Be Heard,* p. 52.

7. Suzette Haden Elgin, *The Last Word on the Gentle Art of Verbal Self-Defense,* p. 24.

8. "Laughter is the Best Medicine," *Reader's Digest,* May 1990, p. 80.

9. David Augsburger, *Caring Enough to Hear and Be Heard,* p. 52.

CHAPTER 6: USE THE "RELATIONS" MODEL FOR EFFECTIVE LISTENING

1. Bernard G. Guerney, Jr., *Relationship Enhancement: Marital/Family Therapist's Manual,* p. 97.

2. Donald Osgood, *Breaking Through,* p. 14.

3. Bernard G. Guerney, Jr., *Relationship Enhancement: Marital/Family Therapist's Manual,* p. 99.

4. Richard Walters, personal interview, November 1982.

5. Bernard G. Guerney, Jr., *Relationship Enhancement: Marital/Family Therapist's Manual,* pp. 100-101.

CHAPTER 7: LEARN TO CONTROL YOUR EMOTIONS WHEN LISTENING

1. Dr. Lyman Steil, Dr. Larry Barker, and Dr. Kitty Watson, *Effective Listening, Key to Your Success,* p. 97.

2. Lee Iacocca, *Iacocca: An Autobiography,* pp. 56-57.

3. Michael Maccoby, *Why Work,* p. 52.

4. Dr. Lyman Steil, personal interview, July 1980 and subsequently.

5. Suzette Haden Elgin, *The Last Word on the Gentle Art of Verbal Self-Defense,* p. 11.

6. Dr. Ralph Nichols, The Institute of Propaganda Analysis described in *Are You Listening?,* pp. 134-136.

7. Paul de Barros, Effective Communication and Development, Inc., *Effective Listening Workshop Workbook,* 1981, p. 32

8. Suzette Haden Elgin, *The Last Word on the Gentle Art of Verbal Self-Defense,* p. 140.

CHAPTER 8: COMMUNISUASION: HOW TO LISTEN PERSUASIVELY

1. Donald V. Siebert, *The Ethical Executive: A Top C.E.O.'s Program for Success with the Corporate World,* p. 37.

2. Richard M. While, Jr., *The Entrepreneur's Manual,* quoted by Alessandra and Wexler in *Non-Manipulative Selling,* p. 5.

3. Donald J. Moine and John H. Herd, *Modern Persuasion Strategies, The Hidden Advantage in Selling,* p. 28.

4. David Augsburger, *Caring Enough to Hear and Be Heard,* p. 65.

5. Vince Pesce, *Siemens-Allise Sales Gram,* Pamphlet, Vol. 1, No. 3, 1984.

6. Suzette Haden Elgin, *The Last Word on the Gentle Art of Verbal Self-Defense,* p. 193.

7. Sigmund Freud, quoted by Alessandra and Wexler in *Non-Manipulative Selling,* p. 96.

8. Joseph Yeager, Eastern Neurolinguistics Programming Institute Lecture, November 1985, New York, New York.

9. Donald J. Moine and John H. Herd, *Modern Persuasion Strategies, The Hidden Advantage in Selling,* p. 66.

10. Moine and Herd, Ibid., p. 60.

11. Jerry Richardson and Joel Margulis, *The Magic of Rapport,* p. 19.

12. Michael McCaskey, "The Hidden Messages Managers Send," *Harvard Business Review,* November/December 1979, p. 147.

13. Robert and Dorothy Bolton, quoted by Wright in *Energize Your Life Through Total Communication,* pp. 69-70.

14. Wright, Ibid., p. 70.

15. Suzette Haden Elgin, *The Last Word on the Gentle Art of Verbal Self-Defense,* p. 209.

16. Donald J. Moine and John H. Herd, *Modern Persuasion Strategies, The Hidden Advantage in Selling,* p. 22.

17. William S. Condon, quoted by Richardson and Margulis in *The Magic of Rapport,* p. 33.

18. Edward T. Hall, quoted by Richardson and Margulis in *The Magic of Rapport,* p. 33.

19. Jurgen Ruesch, professor of psychiatry at the University of California, quoted by Denis Waitley in *The Psychology of Winning,* p. 168.

20. Donald J. Moine and John H. Herd, *Modern Persuasion Strategies, The Hidden Advantage in Selling,* p. 29.

21. Suzette Haden Elgin, *The Last Word on the Gentle Art of Verbal Self-Defense,* p. 194.

22. Anthony Alessandra and Phillip S. Wexler, *Non-Manipulative Selling,* p. 6.

23. Donald J. Moine and John H. Herd, *Modern Persuasion Strategies, The Hidden Advantage in Selling,* p. 20.

CHAPTER 9: PROFIT FROM THE INTERPRETATION OF NONVERBAL COMMUNICATION

1. W. S. Condon, "The Relation of Interactional Synchrony to Cognitive and Emotional Processes," quoted by Elgin in *More on the Gentle Art of Verbal Self-Defense,* p. 219.

2. Elgin, Ibid., p. 220.

3. Elgin, Ibid., p. 216.

4. Elgin, Ibid., p. 203.

5. Dr. Lyman Steil, personal conversation, July 1980.

6. Fred Liedtke, "Humor in Uniform," *Reader's Digest,* May 1981, p. 77.

7. Daniel Coleman, *The New York Times,* April 8, 1986. Report of a research project on nonverbal communication carried out by Peter Blanck and his associates and quoted by Elgin in *Mastering the Gentle Art of Verbal Self-Defense,* p. 52.

8. Paul Ekman and Wallace V. Friesen, *Unmasking the Face: A Guide to Recognizing Emotions from Facial Expressions,* p. 5.

9. Ekman and Friesen, Ibid., p. 5.

10. Ekman and Friesen, Ibid., p. 88.

11. Ekman and Friesen, Ibid., p. 14.

12. Donald Osgood, *Breaking Through,* pp. 30-31.

13. Suzette Haden Elgin, *The Last Word on the Gentle Art of Verbal Self-Defense,* p. 217.

CHAPTER 10: IMPROVE LISTENING THROUGH EFFECTIVE NOTETAKING

1. Dr. Ralph Nichols, *Are You Listening?,* p. 114.

2. Nichols, Ibid., pp. 113-114.

3. Nichols, Ibid., pp. 115-116. In these pages Nichols has an excellent discussion on notetaking.

4. Dr. Lyman Steil, Dr. Larry Barker, and Dr. Kitty Watson, *Effective Listening, Key to Your Success,* pp. 110-114.

5. Steil, Barker, and Watson, Ibid., p. 108.

6. Steil, Barker, and Watson, Ibid., p. 20.

7. Paul de Barros, Effective Communication and Development, Inc., *Effective Listening Workshop Workbook,* 1980, p. 40.

8. de Barros, Ibid., p. 40.

9. Dr. Lyman Steil, provided through the University of Minnesota, original source unknown.

Bibliography

Alessandra, Anthony J. and Phillip S. Wexler with Jerry D. Deen. *Non-Manipulative Selling.* Reston: Reston Publishing Company, 1979.

Augsburger, David. *Caring Enough to Hear and Be Heard.* Scottdale, PA: Herald Press, 1982.

Bandler, Richard and John Grinder. *Frogs into Princes.* Moab, UT: Real People Press, 1979.

Blood Pressure Study, 1979, Society of Actuaries and Association of Life Insurance Medical Directors of America. November 1980.

Boa, Kenneth. Personal conversations, 1981 to 1990.

Burley-Allen, Madelyn. *Listening: The Forgotten Skill.* New York: John Wiley and Sons, Inc, 1982.

Campolo, Anthony, Jr. *The Success Fantasy.* Wheaton: Victor Books, 1980.

de Barros, Paul. Writing assignments for Effective Communication and Development, Inc., 1980 ff.

Delmar, Ken. *Winning Moves.* New York: Warner Books, 1984.

Demaray, Donald E. *Laughter, Joy, and Healing.* Grand Rapids: Baker Book House Company, 1986.

Dobson, James. *Emotions: Can You Trust Them?* Ventura, CA: Gospel Light, 1980.

Ekman, Paul and Wallace V. Friesen. *Unmasking the Face: A Guide to Recognizing Emotions from Facial Expressions.* Palo Alto: Consulting Psychologists Press, 1984.

Elgin, Suzette Haden. *The Last Word on the Gentle Art of Verbal Self-Defense.* Englewood Cliffs: Prentice Hall, Inc., 1980.

Elgin, Suzette Haden. *The Last Word on the Gentle Art of Verbal Self-Defense Workbook.* New York: Dorset, 1987.

Elgin, Suzette Haden. *More on the Gentle Art of Verbal Self-Defense.* Englewood Cliffs: Prentice Hall, Inc., 1983.

Frankl, Viktor E. *Man's Search for Meaning.* New York: Pocket Books, Simon and Schuster, Inc., 1963.

Friedrich, Otto. "What Do Babies Know?" *Time.* August 15, 1983.

Geeting, Baxter and Corinne. *How to Listen Assertively.* New York: Simon and Schuster, 1976.

Glasser, William, Jr., M.D. *Reality Therapy.* New York: Harper and Row, 1965.

Guerney, Bernard G., Jr. *Relationship Enhancement.* San Francisco: Jossey-Bass, Inc., 1977.

Guerney, Bernard G., Jr. *Relationship Enhancement: Marital/ Family Therapist's Manual.* Second Edition. State College, PA: 1976.

Guerney, Bernard G., Jr. *Relationship Enhancement: Marital/ Family Therapy Training Program.* State College, PA: April 1990.

Henry, Lauchland A. *The Professional Guide to Working Smarter.* Tenafly: Berrill-Ellsworth Associates, Inc., 1989.

The Holy Bible. New International Version. New York: Oxford University Press, 1984.

Iacocca, Lee, with William Novak. *Iacocca: An Autobiography.* New York: Bantam Books, 1984.

Keffe, W. F. *Listen Management.* New York: McGraw Hill, 1971.

"Laughter is the Best Medicine." *Reader's Digest.* Pleasantville: May 1990.

Liedtke, Fred. "Humor in Uniform." *Reader's Digest.* Pleasantville: May 1981.

Lynch, James J. *The Language of the Heart.* New York: Basic Books, 1985.

Maccoby, Michael. *Why Work.* New York: Simon and Schuster, 1988.

Maladro, Loretta A. and Dr. Larry Barker. *Non-Verbal Communication.* Reading: Addison-Wesley Publishing Company, 1983.

McCaskey, Michael. "The Hidden Messages Managers Send." *Harvard Business Review.* November/December 1979.

Mehrabian, Albert. *Nonverbal Communication.* Chicago: Aldine-Atherton, 1972.

Moine, Donald J. and John H. Herd. *Modern Persuasion Strategies, The Hidden Advantage in Selling.* Englewood Cliffs: Prentice-Hall, 1984.

Nichols, Ralph G. and Leonard A. Stevens. *Are You Listening?* New York: McGraw-Hill Book Company, Inc., 1957.

Nierenberg, Gerard I. *The Art of Negotiating.* New York: Simon and Schuster, 1968.

Nierenberg, Gerard and Henry H. Calero. *How to Read a Person Like a Book.* New York: Simon and Schuster, 1971.

Osgood, Donald W. *Breaking Through.* Old Tappan: Fleming H. Revell Company, 1986.

Peale, Norman Vincent. *Positive Imaging.* Old Tappan: Fleming H. Revell Company, 1982.

Pesce, Vince. *Seimens-Allise Sales Gram.* Pamphlet, Vol. 1, No 3, 1984.

Peter, Lawrence J. *The Laughter Prescription.* New York: Balantine Books, Random House, Inc., 1982.

Peters, Tom. "Get Physical: Manage Space in Business Life." *Ossining Citizen Register.* December 1989.

Petersen, Roger. Writing assignments for Effective Communication and Development, Inc., 1989 ff.

Richardson, Jerry and Joel Margulis. *The Magic of Rapport.* San Francisco: Harbor Publishing, Inc., 1986.

Robertson, Arthur K. *Effective Listening Workbook.* New York: Effective Communication and Development, Inc., 1988.

Schreiner, Samuel, Jr. "A Question That Can Save Marriages." *Reader's Digest.* Pleasantville: February 1990.

Schuller, Robert H. *Self-Esteem: The New Reformation.* Waco: Word Books, 1982.

Siebert, Donald V. *The Ethical Executive: A Top C.E.O.'s Program for Success with the Corporate World.* New York: Simon and Schuster, 1984.

Simon, Sidney B. *Negative Criticism*. Niles: Argus Communications, 1978.

Smith, Harold. "The 20% Activities That Bring 80% Payoff." *Training Today*. Chicago: American Society for Training & Development, The Chicagoland Chapter, June 1978.

Soundview Executive Book Summaries. Bristol: Soundview Executive Book Summaries, July 1989.

Steil, Lyman K. "A Longitudinal Analysis of Listening Pedagogy in Minnesota Secondary Public Schools." Ph.D. Dissertation, Wayne State University, Detroit, Michigan, 1978.

Steil, Lyman K. Personal conversations, 1980 ff.

Steil, Lyman K., Larry L. Barker, and Kitty W. Watson. *Effective Listening, Key to Your Success*. Reading: Addison-Wesley Publishing Company, Inc., 1983.

Steil, Lyman K., JoAnne Summerfield, and George deMare. *Listening—It Can Change Your Life*. New York: John Wiley and Sons, Inc., 1983.

Waitley, Denis. *The Psychology of Winning*. New York: Berkeley Books, 1984.

Waitley, Denis. *Seeds of Greatness*. New York: Simon and Schuster, 1983.

Waitley, Denis. *The Winner's Edge*. New York: Berkeley Books, 1980.

Walters, Richard. Personal consultation on Listening Workshop, 1981 ff.

Walters, Walter. Personal interview, November 1981.

Wolff, Florence I., Nadine Marsnik, William S. Tacey, and Ralph G. Nichols. *Perceptive Listening*. New York: Holt Rinehart and Winston, 1983.

Wright, H. Norman. *Energize Your Life Through Total Communication*. Old Tappan: Fleming H. Revell Company, 1986.

Yeager, Joseph. Eastern Neurolinguistics Programming Institute, Certification Training, April 1985 to February 1986.

Ziglar, Zig. *Top Performance*. Old Tappan: Fleming H. Revell Company, 1986.

Index